BETROCK'S
GUIDE TO LANDSCAPE
PALMS

Alan W. Meerow

BETROCK'S
GUIDE TO LANDSCAPE
PALMS

Alan W. Meerow

University of Florida — IFAS

BETROCK

Information Systems, Inc.

Cooper City, Florida

1992

First Edition 1992

Published by
Betrock Information Systems, Inc.
10400 Griffin Road, Suite 301
Cooper City, Florida 33328

Library of Congress Cataloging-in-Publication Date
Meerow, Alan W., 1992
Betrock's Guide To Landscape Palms/Alan W. Meerow
Library of Congress #92-072952
ISBN #0-9629761-1-3

Front and Back Cover Photo Credit by William Houghton, Fairchild Tropical Garden
Inside Cover Photo Credit by Brad Miller, The Kentia Palm Company: the Kentia palm, *Howea forsteriana*, in its native habitat on Lord Howe Island, New South Wales, Australia
Typesetting, Page Layout, Production and Line Drawings by Mary B. Feeney

Table of Contents

Acknowledgements...vii

Photo Credits ix

Preface xi

Introduction...xiii

SECTION I

Encyclopedia of Landscape Palms 3

SECTION II

What Is a Palm?.. 107

Fertilizing Palms.. 114

Transplanting and Landscape Care of Palms.. 119

Cold Protection and Treating Cold-Damaged Palms.. 124

Insect Pests of Landscape Palms 125

Disease Problems of Landscape Palms.. 128

Key to Landscape Palms.. 134

SECTION III

USDA Plant Hardiness Zone Map.. 141

Palms Hardy Above USDA Zone 10.. 142

Highly Salt Tolerant Palms.. 142

Highly Drought Tolerant Palms... 142

Palms That Will Grow in Low Light (<500 foot candles)................................ 143

Palms That Will Grow in Part Shade... 143

Fast Growing Palms... 144

Palms Generally 20' Tall or Less... 144

Solitary Palms.. 145

Clustering Palms.. 145

Palms with Spines or Teeth 146

Palms with Irritating Fruit... 146

Index to Common Names and Synonyms 147

Glossary 151

Bibliography 152

About the Author.. 153

Acknowledgements

Numerous colleagues, students, teachers and friends have helped make this book a reality through their enthusiasm, dedication, and love of palms. My present or former colleagues at the University of Florida Fort Lauderdale Research and Education Center, Drs. Timothy K. Broschat, Henry Donselman, Robin Giblin-Davis, Nigel A. Harrison and Forrest W. Howard have enlightened all palm horticulturists with myriad developments in the science of palm horticulture. Donald R. Hodel aided in the accuracy of the information on *Chamaedorea* and donated photographs of a number of species. Chuck Hubbuch and Nancy Edmondson reviewed the manuscript and made invaluable suggestions. In addition, the following people, directly or indirectly, have enriched my own experience of palms and, as a consequence, the value of this book: Dr. Michael Balick, David Bar-Zvi, Libby and Dr. Byron Besse, Dave Besst, Tom and David Capellazo, Dr. Ann Chase, Murray and Deborah Corman, Paul Craft, Dr. John Dransfield, Liz Dunn, Don Evans, Dr. Jack Fisher, Dr. Andrew Henderson, C. Way and Geri Hoyt, Dearmand Hull, Gene Joiner, Bill Jones, David and Agnes McLean, Jack Miller, Sam Mitchell, Richard Moyroud, Chris Olano, Chris Oppenheimer, David Pais, Wes Parrish, Bob Petersen, Dr. Robert Read, Dr. Roger Sanders, Ron and Charlotte Schaff, Jeff and Larry Searle, Dr. Gary Simone, Bill Theobold, Dr. P.B. Tomlinson, Dr. Natalie Uhl, the Vick family, George and Jean Zammas, Dr. Scott Zona. However, all opinions and subjective commentary expressed within these pages are my own and should not be laid at the feet of these individuals. Fairchild Tropical Garden provided inspiration and many of the fine palm specimens pictured in this book.

My sincerest appreciation to Irv and Bette Betrock, Bill and April Hutchinson and Denis Bedu of Betrock Information Systems for their patience and diligence in turning an idea into a reality. Finally, to my wife Linda and my children, Sara and Andrew, who put up with many long nights in front of the computer screen.

Photo Credits

Timothy K. Broschat: pp. 7, 10, 19, 49 (large), 67 (large), 74, 75, 82, 98 (large)

Murray Corman: pp. 31, 68 (inset), 73, 99, 101

James De Filippis: p. 125/Figs. 26-28; p. 126/Figs. 30-31; p. 127/Fig. 36

Robin Giblin-Davis: p. 126/Fig. 29; p. 127/Figs. 32-35

Nigel A. Harrison: p. 117/Fig. 21; p. 128/Figs. 37-38; p. 129/Figs. 40-41; p. 130/Figs. 42-45; p. 131/Figs. 46-49; p. 132/Figs. 51-52

Donald R. Hodel: pp. 13, 14, 21, 22, 23, 25, 26, 28, 53

Forrest W. Howard: p. 15 (large)

Chuck Hubbuck: pp. 8, 18, 46, 58, 71 (large), 72, 86

Gene Joiner: p. 88

Jack Miller: p. 119/Fig. 23; p. 120/Fig. 24

All other photos by the author or Betrock Information Systems, Inc.

Preface

As landscape plants, palms are currently receiving more attention than ever before, a reflection, no doubt, of both the allure of the exotic and the enormous rise in population experienced by areas of the United States where palms can be enjoyed outdoors in great variety. In recent years, more books have appeared about palms than ever before. What has not been available is a concise guide to the most common palms utilized in subtropical and tropical landscapes, providing as much cultural information as is known for each and significant identifying characteristics, in a format accessible to the average home gardener or landscape professional. *Betrock's Guide to Landscape Palms* has been designed to meet that need. In addition to describing the salient characteristics and landscape features of 102 species of palms grown throughout the subtropics and tropics, up-to-date information on the general culture of landscape palms, reflecting current horticultural research, is presented. The author, Dr. Alan Meerow, in just a few short years as Palm and Tropical Ornamentals Specialist for the University of Florida's Institute of Food and Agricultural Sciences, has become recognized throughout Florida for his expertise on these marvelous plants. We at Betrock Information Systems believe that this guide will become a valued addition to the bookshelves of horticultural professionals and enthusiasts in Florida, California, Hawaii, and wherever else palms are grown for their beauty and unique landscape signature.

Irv Betrock, President
Betrock Information Systems

Introduction

Palms are the universal symbol of the tropics in the popular imagination. Swaying coconut palms beckon to winter-weary temperate zone dwellers from the glossy advertisements of tropical beach resorts, while stately date palms guard the ramparts of sun belt housing developments in California, Arizona and Florida. As exotic and inextricably related to pleasure as this mystique may be, it belies the importance of this family of plants that Linnaeus called "Principes," the princes of the plant kingdom. Palms are second only to the grasses or grains in economic importance. Throughout the world's tropics, palms have figured in local and national economies for centuries, even millenia. For some species in fact, virtually every part of the plant has found some use by people: leaves for thatch and fiber, food and oil from the fruits and seed, sugar and intoxicants from the sap, and even trunks for construction. So dependent on palms are certain cultures that the status of a particular species may even rise to the level of deity; certain Amazon tribes revere a particular palm as the giver of all life.

As landscape plants, palms are prized for their unique architecture and the intricate texture and form of their leaves and stems. Their beauty, durability, and variety rank them among the most highly valued of all landscape plants in subtropical and tropical regions. With but a few exceptions, the 102 species covered in detail within these pages represent the most popular and available palms for landscape use in regions of the United States where palms can be grown outdoors. It is intended, however, that this book be useful anywhere in the world where palms are used as exterior landscape plants. A few of the palms treated are not yet widely offered in nurseries but indications are such that they soon will be.

How To Use This Book

This book is divided into three sections. The first section of the book is an encyclopedia of 102 cultivated palm species arranged alphabetically by scientific name. Each species treated is illustrated with at least one color photograph. The text that accompanies the pictures follows a structured format that remains constant throughout the book and which is designed to present descriptive and cultural information about each palm in a simple, easily accessible manner. Overly technical language has been kept to a minimum. Any botanical terminology used in the text is defined in the glossary located on page 151. The second section provides some background about the palm family and detailed information on the cultivation of landscape palms including fertilization, transplanting, landscape use and maintenance, pests, diseases and other problems encountered by palms. The third section of the book consists of lists of palms with particular landscape tolerances and an index to all the palms treated arranged alphabetically by common names and incorrect scientific name (synonyms). This should allow the reader to locate a species within the text even if he or she knows only a common name or incorrect scientific name for it.

An identification key to the palms treated in the book can be found on page 134. This key relies on only characters of leaf, stem or habit and should be usable by anyone with the most basic understanding of plant form.

Data referring to landscape tolerances such as drought tolerance, light requirements, etc. are based on expectations for the species in a warm, subtropical or tropical humid climate. In locations such as California, many of the palms listed as highly drought tolerant will require supplemental irrigation during that state's long, rainless summer season. Likewise, some of the palms whose light requirements are listed as "moderate" (a number of *Chamaedorea* spp., for example) are able to withstand full sun in coastal California's cool climate.

The following are brief explanatory notes about the data fields used throughout the encyclopedia:

Scientific Name: The universally accepted botanical name (genus and species) for the palm, followed by a pronunciation guide. The pronunciations, while not formatted using official phonetic symbols, are designed to easily indicate the accepted way to pronounce the scientific names used in this book. Vowels with a (-) over them are pronounced like the name of that particular letter. For example ā is pronounced "ay," ī is pronounced "eye." The syllable that is stressed in each name is indicated by **boldface**.

Common Name: One or more widely used vernacular names for the palm in the English speaking world.

Subfamily: The subdivision of the palm family to which the particular species belongs (see "Classification of the Palm Family," page 113).

Tribe: A further subdivision of the subfamily to which the particular species belongs (see "Classification of the Palm Family," page 113).

Origin: The part of the world to which the particular species is native.

Hardiness Zone: The range of climate zones in which the palm can be grown successfully, based on the USDA Plant Hardiness Zone Map (see page 141). It should be kept in mind that during unusually severe winters, some species normally suitable for a particular zone may be injured or even killed.

Typical Height: The average expected height or height range that the species can be expected to reach. However. the actual height that the palm will achieve will vary due to environmental and cultural conditions.

Growth Rate: The relative rate of growth of the species. **Slow** indicates annual growth of less than 1 foot. **Moderate** refers to annual growth of 1-3 feet. **Fast** indicates yearly growth increments of more than 3 feet. Again, the actual growth rate exhibited will vary depending on the conditions received in cultivation.

LANDSCAPE CHARACTERISTICS

Salt Tolerance: The palm's relative tolerance of salt, whether from spray received by the leaves or saline water in the root zone. **Low** indicates that the palm is largely intolerant of salt on the roots or leaves; **moderate** refers to palms that will require protection from direct spray and intensely saline water but can tolerant mildly brackish water and some incidental spray; **high** indicates a palm that can be planted in exposed seaside locations.

Drought Tolerance: The palm's relative ability to persist and grow without supplementary irrigation ONCE ESTABLISHED. **Low** indicates that the palm will require regular irrigation during periods of no rainfall; **moderate** refers to a palm that will require occasional irrigation during dry periods; **high** refers to a palm that can survive periods of drought without supplemental irrigation. THESE CATEGORIES ARE BASED ON A WARM, HUMID, SUBTROPICAL CLIMATE WITH RAINFALL DISTRIBUTED THROUGHOUT THE YEAR BUT HIGHEST DURING THE WARMEST MONTHS, AND CANNOT ALWAYS BE APPLIED TO MORE ARID REGIONS.

Soil Requirements: The type of soil most suitable to the palm. **Acid** refers to soils with a pH of less than 7.0; **alkaline** refers to a soil with a pH higher than 7.0; **well-drained** refers to a soil that does not remain water-logged; **widely adaptable** indicates a palm with a broad tolerance of soil types.

Light Requirements: The relative light exposures suitable for the palm. **Low** refers to deep shade (less than 500 foot candles); **moderate** signifies part shade (500-5000 foot candles); **high** refers to light intensities of 5000 foot candles to full sun. Light tolerance may increase for some species when planted in climates where high temperatures remain moderate.

Nutritional Requirements: The relative fertilization needs of the palm. **Low** signifies a palm that requires no supplementary fertilization under typical landscape conditions; **moderate** indicates a palm requiring periodic light fertilization for good growth; **high** refers to palms that must receive regular fertilization in order to prosper.

Uses: The way in which the palm can be used in the landscape.

Propagation: The way in which the palm is increased. For most palms, seed is the only means of propagation, and germination times are indicated.

Human Hazards: Indicates whether the palm presents any danger of injury, either due to spines or teeth present on some of its parts, or the presence of a skin irritant in the fruit.

Major Pest Problems: Insects or mites that frequently attack the palm.

Major Disease or Physiological Problems: Common diseases or other disorders that affect the palm.

Cultivars: Named varieties of the palm that are available in addition to the "typical" form. Most cultivated palms do not have recognized varieties.

Comments: Miscellaneous information about the palm, including at times brief descriptions of related species.

MORPHOLOGY (Identifying Characteristics)

Habit: Whether the palm is **solitary** (single-stemmed) or **clustering** (multiple-stemmed) and the number of leaves usually carried by each stem.

Trunk or Stem Characteristics: Salient identifying characteristics of the palm stem.

Leaf Type: A description of leaf shape and form (see Glossary, page 151 and "What Is A Palm?", page 107).

Foliage Color: A description of leaf color.

Leaf Size: Dimensions of the palm leaf.

Petiole: Size and description of the leaf stem.

Crownshaft: Whether a true crownshaft formed by tightly sheathing leaf bases is present, and, if so, its distinctive features.

Inflorescence: A description of the form, position and size of the flowers stalks.

Gender: How sex is expressed in the flowers of the species. Some palms have bisexual flowers (male and female sex organs in the same flower); some have separate male and female flowers on the same flower stalk (monoecious); and others have separate male and female plants (dioecious).

Flower Color: Color of the flowers.

Fruit Size: Size of the fruit.

Fruit Color: Color of the fruit.

Irritant: Whether the fruit contains calcium oxalate crystals that irritate the skin if the ripe fruit is handled without protection.

SECTION I

ENCYCLOPEDIA OF LANDSCAPE PALM SPECIES

Scientific Name: *Acoelorrhaphe wrightii* (ah-see-lo-ra-fe rite-e-i)
Common Name(s): Paurotis palm, Everglades palm

Typical Height: 20'
Subfamily: Coryphoideae
Tribe: Corypheae

Hardiness Zone: 9B-11
Growth Rate: Slow
Origin: Florida and Caribbean region

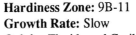

Landscape Characteristics

Salt Tolerance: Moderate
Drought Tolerance: Moderate
Soil Requirements: Widely adaptable
Light Requirements: Moderate, high
Nutritional Requirements: Moderate
Uses: Multi-trunked specimen tree
Propagation: Seed, germinating in 2-3 months; division
Human Hazards: Spiny
Major Pest Problems: None
Major Disease or Physiological Problems:
Manganese deficiency, ganoderma, stigmina leaf spot, graphiola false smut

Morphology (Identifying Characteristics)

Habit: Clustering; each stem bearing 20-30 leaves
Trunk or Stem Characteristics: Slender; persistent leaf bases and fiber
Leaf Type: Palmate, induplicate; divided to more than 1/2 into many narrow segments
Foliage Color: Green; silvery-green below
Leaf Size: 3' wide; segments 1" wide
Petiole: Armed with marginal teeth, 3' long
Crownshaft: None
Inflorescence: From among the leaves; branched; 3-4' long, turning orange in fruit
Gender: Bisexual flowers
Flower Color: White
Fruit Size: 1/2"
Fruit Color: Black
Irritant: No

Comments: The paurotis palm is a distinctive part of the Florida Everglades flora where it frequently forms dense stands at the border of tree islands. It is one of the few cultivated palms that will tolerate poorly drained sites in the landscape. It prefers relatively moist soils; on drier soils growth will be particularly slow. On high pH soils, paurotis palms will manifest manganese deficiency ("frizzletop") unless fertilized regularly with manganese sulfate or a complete fertlizer containing managnese. Paurotis palm will, in time, form a large cluster that restricts its use to sites where such spread will not be a problem.

Scientific Name: *Acrocomia aculeata* (ak-rō-cō-mē-ah ah-qū-lē-**ah**-tah)
Common Name(s): Macaw palm

Typical Height: 30'
Subfamily: Arecoideae
Tribe: Cocoeae

Hardiness Zone: 10A-11
Growth Rate: Slow
Origin: Martinique and Dominica

Salt Tolerance: Moderate
Drought Tolerance: High
Soil Requirements: Widely adaptable
Light Requirements: High
Nutritional Requirements: Moderate
Uses: Specimen tree
Propagation: Seed germinating in 4-6 months after scarification
Human Hazards: Spiny
Major Pest Problems: None
Major Disease or Physiological Problems: Ganoderma

Morphology (Identifying Characteristics)

Habit: Solitary; canopy of 20-30 leaves
Trunk or Stem Characteristics: Smooth, spiny (especially when young), closely ringed, sometimes bulging towards middle
Leaf Type: Pinnately compound, reduplicate; over 300 leaflets
Foliage Color: Green, pale with whitish hairs on underside of leaflets
Leaf Size: 10-12' long; leaflets about 3' long, 2" wide
Petiole: 3' long, spiny
Crownshaft: None
Inflorescence: 5-7 feet long with a large, persistent woody spathe
Gender: Separate male and female flowers on same inflorescence
Flower Color: Yellow
Fruit Size: 2"
Fruit Color: Light green
Irritant: No

Comments: Despite the vicious spines on the trunk and leaf stalks, the macaw palm makes a striking landscape specimen where space allows. In aspect, it suggests a very robust, spiny queen palm. These palms are natives of open, dry and often rocky areas throughout their range, occurring on well-drained sandy soils. Consequently, they are well adapted to seasonally dry tropical areas. Local people use the pith from the stems as a source of starch for themselves and their livestock. An alcoholic beverage is often fermented from the pith as well. Twine is prepared from the leaflets, and the seed is a source of good quality palm oil. However, due to its ferocious armament, the macaw palm remains largely a palm for the collector.

Other Species: *A. totai* (grugru palm), from Paraguay, Argentina and Bolivia, is similar in aspect to the macaw palm but smaller in all parts. Some scientists consider many recognized *Acrocomia* species to be mere variants of *A. aculeata*.

Scientific Name: *Allagoptera arenaria* (a-lah-**gop**-ter-ah ah-ren-**nare**-ē-yah)

Common Name(s): Seashore palm

Typical Height: 4-8'
Subfamily: Arecoideae
Tribe: Cocoeae

Hardiness Zone: 9B-11
Growth Rate: Slow
Origin: Brazil

Landscape Characteristics

Salt Tolerance: High
Drought Tolerance: High
Soil Requirements: Widely adaptable
Light Requirements: High
Nutritional Requirements: Low
Uses: Seaside landscapes, shrub
Propagation: Seed, germinating in 3 months; may not retain viability for long
Human Hazards: None
Major Pest Problems: None
Major Disease or Physiological Problems: Slight susceptibility to lethal yellowing

Morphology (Identifying Characteristics)

Habit: Clustering (with time); each stem bearing 16-20 leaves
Trunk or Stem Characteristics: Trunkless
Leaf Type: Pinnately compound, reduplicate; about 40 leaflets in radiating groups of three that give a plume-like appearance
Foliage Color: Green above, silvery below
Leaf Size: 3-4 feet long; leaflets about 10" long, 1/2-3/4" wide
Petiole: 1-1.5 feet long; unarmed
Crownshaft: None
Inflorescence: Short, unbranched, dense spike with a woody spathe
Gender: Male and female flowers on the same inflorescence
Flower Color: Greenish-yellow
Fruit Size: 1"
Fruit Color: Yellowish-green, ripening to orange
Irritant: No

Comments: In its native habitat in coastal Brazil, the seashore palm grows on primary dunes where constant salt exposure is assured. This fact alone makes it an extremely valuable addition to the landscape palm inventory. This shrubby palm slowly forms a short mound of graceful, plume-like leaves that can be massed effectively or used as a single accent with other extremely salt tolerant plants. The leaflets are situated on the rachis in groups of three, with each radiating outward in a different direction, thus lending the leaves a full, foxtail like quality. The silvery undersides of the leaves are eye-catching in even the slightest sea breeze. The unusual spike-like inflorescences are usually lost among the clusters of leaves. In inland areas, seashore palm does equally well, where its adaptation to beachfront soils allow it to thrive with neglible supplementary fertilization. Seashore palm is at least as hardy as queen palm, and should be trialed further north along the coast in Florida and California.

Scientific Name: *Archontophoenix alexandrae* (ark-on-tō-fē-nix   ah-lex-ann-drē)
Common Name(s): Alexandra palm, King Alexander palm

Typical Height: 40'
Subfamily: Arecoideae
Tribe: Areceae

Hardiness Zone: 10B-11
Growth Rate: Moderate
Origin: Australia

Landscape Characteristics

Salt Tolerance: Low
Drought Tolerance: Moderate
Soil Requirements: Widely adaptable
Light Requirements: Moderate, high
Nutritional Requirements: Moderate
Uses: Specimen tree
Propagation: Seed, germinating in 6 weeks to 3 months; best sown fresh
Human Hazards: None
Major Pest Problems: None
Major Disease or Physiological Problems: Transplant shock if poorly handled, phytophthora bud rot, fungal leaf spots
Cultivars: 'Mt. Lewis' has a brownish-red crownshaft; 'Kuranda' has a broader trunk than typical

Morphology (Identifying Characteristics)

Habit: Solitary; canopy of 8-12 leaves
Trunk or Stem Characteristics: Light gray, ridged leaf scars, swollen base
Leaf Type: Pinnately compound, reduplicate; 100 or more leaflets
Foliage Color: Light green above, grayish-white below
Leaf Size: 6-10'long, leaflets about 3' long, 2" wide
Petiole: Short, .5-1' long, unarmed
Crownshaft: Smooth; variable in color, from light green to purplish or dull red
Inflorescence: Short, with numerous pendant branches
Gender: Male and female flowers on the same inflorescence
Flower Color: White
Fruit Size: 1/2"
Fruit Color: Red
Irritant: No

Comments: The alexandra palm makes a stately accent in the landscape and works well as a single specimen or a group of several. It is sometimes confused with hurricane palm (*Dictyosperma album*) but can be differentiated by the swollen base, smooth (rather than waxy) crownshaft, shorter leaves, and pendulous inflorescence. New leaves may emerge light bronze in color on young specimens which make attractive container plants (but do not adapt well to very low light). Alexandra palm performs better in the landscape when supplementary irrigation is provided during periods of sustained drought. Likewise, fertilization should be received a minumum of twice per year to prevent disfiguring nutritional deficiencies. Dry winds may also cause some leaf-tip burn. Unfortunately, this species has the reputation for moving poorly from field nurseries. The heart is susceptible to fatal shattering if the crown of the palm is subjected to undue stresses during lifting and transport to the landscape site. Consequently, field grown specimens should be handled very carefully during transplanting. Splinting or otherwise supporting the crown during transportation may be advisable.

Scientific Name: *Archontophoenix cunninghamiana* (ark-on-tō-fē-nix cun-ing-ham-ē-ann-ah)

Common Name(s): Piccabeen palm, Bangalow palm

Typical Height: 30'
Subfamily: Arecoideae
Tribe: Areceae

Hardiness Zone: 10A-11
Growth Rate: Moderate
Origin: Australia

Landscape Characteristics

Salt Tolerance: Low
Drought Tolerance: Moderate
Soil Requirements: Widely adaptable
Light Requirements: Moderate, high
Nutritional Requirements: Moderate
Uses: Specimen tree
Propagation: Seed, germinating in 6 weeks to 3 months; best sown fresh
Human Hazards: None
Major Pest Problems: None
Major Disease or Physiological Problems: Fungal leaf spots

Morphology (Identifying Characteristics)

Habit: Solitary; canopy of 8-12 leaves
Trunk or Stem Characteristics: Slightly swollen at base; ridged leaf scars
Leaf Type: Pinnately compound, reduplicate; over 100 leaflets
Foliage Color: Green on both sides; brown woolly scales on underside near midrib
Leaf Size: 8-10' long; leaflets to 3' long, about 2" wide
Petiole: Short, .5-1' long, unarmed
Crownshaft: Smooth, rusty brown to dull purple
Inflorescence: Numerous 3-4' long pendulous branches
Gender: Separate male and female flowers on the same inflorescence
Flower Color: Pale lavender to purple
Fruit Size: 1/2"
Fruit Color: Pink to red
Irritant: No

Comments: The piccabeen palm is slightly more cold hardy than its relative, *A. alexandreae*, and usually does not grow as tall. It be can differentiated from the latter by its lack of grayish wax on the leaf underside, less swollen trunk base, frequently colored crown-shaft, lilac-colored flowers, and much less strongly ribbed leaflets. The leaves of the piccabeen palm tend to be more lax than the King Alexander, giving it a slightly less formal appearance. Its cultural requirements and landscape use are similar, however.

Scientific Name: *Areca catechu* (ah-rēk-ah cat-eh-chū)
Common Name(s): Betelnut palm

Typical Height: 30'
Subfamily: Arecoideae
Tribe: Areceae

Hardiness Zone: 11
Growth Rate: Moderate
Origin: India through Southeast Asia, Malaysia and Pacific (exact origin uncertain)

Landscape Characteristics

Salt Tolerance: Low
Drought Tolerance: Low
Soil Requirements: Acid best
Light Requirements: Moderate, high
Nutritional Requirements: Moderate
Uses: Specimen tree; interiorscape
Propagation: Seed, germinating in 2-3 months
Human Hazards: None
Major Pest Problems: None
Major Disease or Physiological Problems:
Ganoderma
Cultivars: Possibly regional cultivars in Asia

Morphology (Identifying Characteristics)

Habit: Solitary; canopy of about a dozen leaves
Trunk or Stem Characteristics: Slender, smooth, green (eventually gray) with prominent, wide, white ring scars
Leaf Type: Pinnately compound, reduplicate, arching; with several dozen broad, obliquely toothed leaflets, the terminal two forming a fishtail shape
Foliage Color: Bright green
Leaf Size: 6-8' long; leaflets 1-2' long, 3-6" wide
Petiole: Short, unarmed
Crownshaft: Bright green
Inflorescence: About 3' long, borne below the crownshaft, much branched, the branches straight and thin
Gender: Separate male and female flowers on the same inflorescence
Flower Color: Yellowish-white, fragrant
Fruit Size: 2" long
Fruit Color: Orange or red
Irritant: No, but seeds contain narcotic compounds

Comments: The betelnut palm, immortalized by Bloody Mary in the Rogers and Hammerstein musical "South Pacific," has been spread throughout tropical Asia and the Pacific where it is cultivated for the food storage tissue (endosperm) inside the seed. When chewed with leaves of a pepper vine (*Piper betle*) and ground lime, a narcotic stimulant is released. Prolonged use stains the gums and teeth red. The palm itself makes a lovely specimen with its boldly ringed trunk and smooth green crownshaft, but is very cold sensitive. Young specimens are quite tolerant of shaded conditions.

Other Species: *A. triandra* (East and Southeast Asia) is a clustering species with thinner trunks but otherwise an appearance similar to the betelnut palm. It perfers a shaded location. *A. vestiaria* (eastern Indonesia) is a beautiful clustering species with slender brown trunks, stilt roots, and a stunning orange-red crownshaft.

Scientific Name: *Arenga tremula* (ah-**rang**-ah treh-mū-lah)
Common Name(s): Dwarf sugar palm

Typical Height: 6-12'
Subfamily: Arecoideae
Origin: Phillipines

Hardiness Zone: 10A-11
Growth Rate: Moderate
Tribe: Caryoteae

Landscape Characteristics

Salt Tolerance: Low
Drought Tolerance: Moderate
Soil Requirements: Widely adaptable
Light Requirements: Moderate, high
Nutritional Requirements: Moderate
Uses: Shrub, screen, specimen plant
Propagation: Seed, often germinating unevenly; division
Human Hazards: Irritant
Major Pest Problems: None
Major Disease or Physiological Problems: Graphiola false smut

Comments: *Arenga tremula* and the related *A. engleri* are hardier and much more useful as landscape plants than the economically important *A. pinnata*. Though the individual stems die after fruiting, new stems continue to arise from the base. Both are clustering and low-growing, and can be utilized as screening plants.

Morphology (Identifying Characteristics)

Habit: Clustering; each stem with 8-10 leaves; each stem dies after fruiting
Trunk or Stem Characteristics: Slender, clean, distinctly ringed
Leaf Type: Pinnately compound, induplicate, arching; usually with over 100 mostly 2-ranked leaflets inconspicuously toothed at points along margins
Foliage Color: Dark green above, pale green below
Leaf Size: 7-13' long; leaflets 2-3' long, 1.25" wide
Petiole: 2-3' long, unarmed
Crownshaft: None
Inflorescence: 4' long, held high above the foliage
Gender: Separate male and female flowers on the same inflorescence
Flower Color: Green **Fruit Size:** 1/2"
Fruit Color: Red **Irritant:** Yes

Other Species: *A. engleri* (Taiwan) is probably the hardiest species in the genus (to Zone 9B). It grows slightly smaller than *A. tremula*, with fiber-covered stems and leaflets that are silvery on the underside. The short flower stalks are hidden among the leaves and the orange flowers are fragrant. The sugar palm, *A. pinnata*, is a solitary species that produces an erect crown of very large (over 20' long) leaves and fibrous spines on the trunk. At about 20 years of age it begins to flower, fruit and die. It is cultivated as a primary source of sugar throughout eastern Asia. The juice is collected from cut flower stalks and boiled down into sugar or fermented into an alcoholic beverage. The moisture resistant fibers were once very important in manufacturing but have been supplanted by synthetics. The fruits of all *Arenga* species contain high concentrations of irritating calcium oxalate crystals.

Scientific Name: *Bactris gasipaes* (bak-tris gas-eh-pēz)
Common Name(s): Peach palm, Pejibaye

Typical Height: 25'
Subfamily: Arecoideae
Tribe: Cocoeae

Hardiness Zone: 10B-11
Growth Rate: Moderate
Origin: Central and South America (exact origin unknown)

Landscape Characteristics

Salt Tolerance: Low
Drought Tolerance: Moderate
Soil Requirements: Acid
Light Requirements: Moderate, high
Nutritional Requirements: Moderate to high
Uses: Specimen tree, edible fruit
Propagation: Seed, germinating in 2 or more months; division
Human Hazards: Spiny
Major Pest Problems: None
Major Disease or Physiological Problems: None
Cultivars: Numerous local varieties in Central and South America

Morphology (Identifying Characteristics)

Habit: Clustering, rarely solitary, with 5-6 stems each bearing 8-12 leaves
Trunk or Stem Characteristics: Light brown; spines between the wide, circling ring scars
Leaf Type: Pinnately compound, reduplicate; with about 4 dozen pointed, drooping leaflets arranged in groups of 2-5, the terminal leaflets largest
Foliage Color: Light green
Leaf Size: 8-12' long; leaflets 2' long, 1.25" wide
Petiole: 5' long, spiny, especially at base; somes spines on rachis
Crownshaft: None
Inflorescence: 1-5' long; borne from among the lower leaves, pendulous, branched once
Gender: Separate male and female flowers on the same inflorescence
Flower Color: Yellowish-white
Fruit Size: 2" diameter
Fruit Color: Orange-yellow
Irritant: No; edible

Comments: Palms as spiny as the 200 or more species of *Bactris* are rarely favored for landscaping, and it is doubtful that any member of this large, primarily rain forest, genus will soon be encountered more widely than as an occasional curiosity in botanical or collectors' gardens. The single species treated here is important because of its highly valued fruit, an important food source throughout Central and South America where it is cultivated widely. In fact, the exact nativity of peach palm is unknown, and the species is seen only in cultivation. The large fruits must first be boiled in salt water to be rendered edible. So prepared, they have a mealy texture, rich in oil, with a flavor pleasant (or at least inoffensive) to most palates.

Scientific Name: *Bismarckia nobilis* (biz-mark-ē-ah nō-bil-is)
Common Name(s): Bismarck palm

Typical Height: 30-60'
Subfamily: Coryphoideae
Tribe: Borasseae

Hardiness Zone: 10A-11
Growth Rate: Slow (towards moderate after trunk development)
Origin: Madagascar

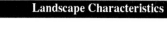

Landscape Characteristics

Salt Tolerance: Moderate
Drought Tolerance: High
Soil Requirements: Widely adaptable
Light Requirements: Moderate, high
Nutritional Requirements: Moderate
Uses: Specimen tree
Propagation: Seeds, often germinating in less than 2 months
Human Hazards: None
Major Pest Problems: None
Major Disease or Physiological Problems: None

Morphology (Identifying Characteristics)

Habit: Solitary, massive; canopy of 20-30 leaves
Trunk or Stem characteristics: Leaf bases adhere when young, later gray and fissured; often swollen at base
Leaf Type: Costapalmate, induplicate, stiff and upright; divided to about 1/3 into approximately 20 segments; lop-sided hastula
Foliage Color: Blue-green to bronze-green, slight red edge, waxy
Leaf Size: To 10' in diameter
Petiole: Waxy, stout, 4-8' long; winged at base and very sparsely toothed at edge
Crownshaft: None
Inflorescence: 4' long; branched; ultimate branches thick and catkin-like
Gender: Separate male and female plants
Flower Color: Cream
Fruit Size: 1.5"
Fruit Color: Brown
Irritant: No

Comments: *Bismarckia* is one of the most beautiful and desirable fan palms for use in subtropical landscapes. Its bold and formal appearance dominates the area it inhabits. *Bismarckia* is particularly well-adapted to Florida conditions, and with only moderate fertilization the palm remains free of nutritional deficiencies. The bismarck palm is massive in aspect; even relatively young specimens may spread to 20' or more. Consequently, this beautiful palm is out-of-scale for small residential yards, and may make a small house appear even smaller. *Bismarckia* transplants with some difficulty, and it is one of the few palms that are regularly root-pruned in field nurseries. The loss of several older leaves is not infrequent shortly after installation. Young palms (before trunk development) are especially intolerant of being moved due to the burial and underground development of the seedling stem and should only be transplanted out of containers. Bismarcks have been used as far north as Sarasota along the Florida coast; freeze damage occurs but the palm generally recovers in a single season of growth.

Scientific Name: *Borassus flabellifer* (bō-ras-sus flah-bell-eh-fer)
Common Name(s): Palmyra palm, Lontar palm

Typical Height: 50-70'
Subfamily: Coryphoideae
Tribe: Borasseae

Hardiness Zone: 10B-11
Growth Rate: Slow (moderate after trunk development)
Origin: India, but widely distributed throughout tropical Asia

Landscape Characteristics

Salt Tolerance: Moderate
Drought Tolerance: High
Soil Requirements: Widely adaptable
Light Requirements: High
Nutritional Requirements: Low
Uses: Specimen tree, edible fruit
Propagation: Seed, germinating slowly over 6-12 months; very deep rooted
Human Hazards: Spiny
Major Pest Problems: None
Major Disease or Physiological Problems: Moderate susceptibility to lethal yellowing, phytophthora bud rot
Cultivars: Though regional varieties exist, few if any have been formally recognized. Interestingly, some authorities consider the other 4-6 species of *Borassus* to be variants of the palmyra palm.

Morphology (Identifying Characteristics)

Habit: Solitary, massive; canopy of 2-3 dozen or more leaves
Trunk or Stem Characteristics: Gray, smooth or rough, ringed, covered with split leaf bases when young, swollen at base and sometimes also above middle
Leaf Type: Costapalmate, induplicate, stiff and somewhat folded, divided into 60-80 segments that split at their tips
Foliage Color: Gray-green to blue-green
Leaf Size: 6-10' wide; segments 3-5' long, 4" wide
Petiole: 3-5' long, stout; armed with broad, black teeth at margin
Crownshaft: None
Inflorescence: 4-6' long with short branches, branches of male flowers particularly thick; borne from among the leaves
Gender: Separate male and female plants
Flower Color: Cream
Fruit Size: 6-8" diameter
Fruit Color: Brown
Irritant: No; edible

Comments: This magnificent fan palm has been cultivated by humans for millenia, and rivals the coconut in importance to some local economies in Asia. Some biblical scholars have even suggested that the "apple" of which Adam and Eve partook in Eden was probably the fruit of the palmyra palm. Virtually every part of the palmyra palm has found a use, from the large, sturdy leaves as thatch, to the sweet tasting fruit, eaten raw or cooked. The large inflorescences are tapped for their copious juice which is then condensed into palm sugar or fermented into alcoholic toddy. Palmyras grow in hot, monsoon regions and can form large populations in the wild. They are equally at home in forested and open habitats. The distribution of this species has no doubt been heavily influenced by mankind. Germinating seedlings descend for many feet below ground before any growth emerges above the surface. The palmyra thrives in any moist, warm, tropical climate, though its ultimate size and spread limits its landscape utility.

Scientific Name: *Brahea armata* (bra-hē-ah are-**mah**-tah)
Common Name(s): Blue hesper palm

Typical Height: 30-40'
Subfamily: Coryphoideae
Tribe: Corypheae

Hardiness Zone: 9B-11
Growth Rate: Slow
Origin: Baja California

Landscape Characteristics

Salt Tolerance: Moderate
Drought Tolerance: High
Soil Requirements: Alkaline
Light Requirements: High
Nutritional Requirements: Low
Uses: Specimen tree
Propagation: Seed, germinating in 2-3 months
Human Hazards: Spiny
Major Pest Problems: Palmetto weevils
Major Disease or Physiological Problems:
Phytophthora root and bud rots

Morphology (Identifying Characteristics)

Habit: Solitary, robust; canopy of 50-60 leaves
Trunk or Stem Characteristics: Thick, swollen at base, covered with a shag of dead leaves, eventually gray and ringed
Leaf Type: Costapalmate, induplicate, very stiff, folded; divided about halfway into 30-40 tapered segments that split at their tips
Foliage Color: Blue-green, very waxy
Leaf Size: 6-8' wide; segments 3-4' long, 2" wide
Petiole: 5' long, armed with downward pointing teeth; waxy below
Crownshaft: None
Inflorescence: To 15' long, borne among and extending far beyond the leaves; shortly branched, the ultimate branchlets hairy
Gender: Bisexual flowers
Flower Color: Yellow
Fruit Size: 1" long
Fruit Color: Yellow with brown stripes
Irritant: No

Comments: Blue hesper palm prospers in southern California, where, despite its slow growth rate, it is prized for its dramatic canopy of ice-blue leaves and long inflorescences. In moist subtropical and tropical climates such as Florida, the palm grows poorly and is short-lived. Magnificent specimens of blue hesper palm and other *Brahea* species can be seen at Huntington Botanical Garden in Los Angeles.

Scientific Name: *Brahea edulis* (bra-hē-ah ed-ūl-is)
Common Name(s): Guadalupe palm

Typical Height: 30'
Subfamily: Coryphoideae
Tribe: Corypheae

Hardiness Zone: 10A-11
Growth Rate: Slow
Origin: Guadalupe Island (off west coast of Mexico)

Landscape Characteristics

Salt Tolerance: Moderate
Drought Tolerance: High
Soil Requirements: Alkaline
Light Requirements: High
Nutritional Requirements: Low
Uses: Specimen tree, edible fruit
Propagation: Seed germinating in 2-4 months
Human Hazards: Spiny (variable)
Major Pest Problems: Palmetto weevils
Major Disease or Physiological Problems:
Phytophthora root and bud rots

Morphology (Identifying Characteristics)

Habit: Solitary, robust; canopy of several dozen leaves
Trunk or Stem Characteristics: Brown, ringed
Leaf Type: Costapalmate, induplicate, stiffly folded; divided about halfway into 70-80 segments that split deeply at tips
Foliage Color: Green on both sides
Leaf Size: 3-6' wide; segments 3-4' long, 1" wide
Petiole: 4-5' long, with or without teeth on margin
Crownshaft: None
Inflorescence: 4-5' long, borne from among the leaves
Gender: Bisexual flowers
Flower Color: Yellow
Fruit Size: 1"
Fruit color: Black
Irritant: No; in fact, they are sweet and edible

Comments: Guadalupe palm does not make quite as striking a specimen as the blue hesper palm, but does have the distinction of producing an edible fruit. As with all *Brahea* species, humid tropical climates do not suit the Guadalupe palm.

Typical Height: 15'
Subfamily: Arecoideae
Tribe: Cocoeae

Hardiness Zone: 8-10B
Growth Rate: Slow
Origin: Central-southern Brazil and contiguous Argentina and Uruguay

Landscape Characteristics

Salt Tolerance: Moderate
Drought Tolerance: High
Soil Requirements: Widely adaptable
Light Requirements: Moderate, high
Nutritional Requirements: Moderate
Uses: Small tree, edible fruit
Propagation: Seed, germinating in six months or more, faster after dry storage
Human Hazards: Spiny
Major Pest Problems: Scales
Major Disease or Physiological Problems: Ganoderma, stigmina leaf spot, graphiola false smut, phytophthora bud rot

Morphology (Identifying Characteristics)

Habit: Solitary; canopy of 40-50 leaves
Trunk or Stem Characteristics: Thick, covered with overlapping, stubby and woody leaf bases for many years
Leaf Type: Pinnately compound, reduplicate, stiffly arching, with numerous leaflets
Foliage Color: Blue-green
Leaf Size: 4-6' long; leaflets about 2.5' long, 1" wide
Petiole: 4-6' long, with slender, fibrous spines on margins
Crownshaft: None
Inflorescence: 3-4' long; once-branched
Gender: Separate male and female flowers on the same inflorescence
Flower Color: Creamy yellow to reddish
Fruit Size: 1"
Fruit Color: Yellow to orange
Irritant: No; edible

Comments: Pindo palm is the hardiest feather-leafed palm currently in wide cultivation. It is used throughout the northern half of Florida as a specimen plant, functioning well in median and even avenue plantings, despite its relatively small stature. Its performance is best above USDA Zone 10B, and it is reputedly hardy into the Carolinas. The arching, blue-green leaves are crowded with many upward pointing leaflets that form a pronounced V-shape. The species is considerably variable in nature, the forms differing in ultimate height, trunk thickness, leaf color and amount of arching, and fruit color and taste. The best quality pindo fruits are very sweet with a flavor some find reminescent of a pineapple/banana mixture. They make a tasty jelly. *Butia* hybridizes readily with its close relative the queen palm (*Syagrus romanzoffiana*) and such hybrids, intermediate in morphology and hardiness, are occasionally offered by nurseries.

Other Species: *B. yatay* is similar in appearance and hardiness but with more widely spreading leaves. *B. eriospatha* has shorter, bright green leaves and leaf bases covered with brown hair.

Scientific Name: *Carpentaria acuminata* (car-pen-**tare**-ē-ah ak-ū-min-**ah**-tah)
Common Name(s): Carpentaria palm

Typical Height: 40'
Subfamily: Arecoideae
Tribe: Areceae

Hardiness Zone: 10B-11
Growth Rate: Fast
Origin: Australia

Landscape Characteristics

Salt Tolerance: Low
Drought Tolerance: Low
Soil Requirements: Widely adaptable
Light Requirements: High
Nutritional Requirements: Moderate
Uses: Specimen tree
Propagation: Seed, which germinate readily when fresh in 1-3 months
Human Hazards: Irritant
Major Pest Problems: Thrips
Major Disease or Physiological Problems:
Trunk rot, possibly related to cold damage

Morphology (Identifying Characteristics)

Habit: Solitary; canopy of 10-12 leaves
Trunk or Stem Characteristics: Slender, smooth, gray, widely-spaced rings
Leaf Type: Pinnately compound, reduplicate; up to 100 broad leaflets with 1-2 teeth on lower edge; uppermost and lowermost pair of leaflets widest
Foliage Color: Deep green above, waxy blue-green below
Leaf Size: 5-6' long; leaflets about 2' long, 1.5" wide
Petiole: Short, about 1' long, unarmed; some brown woolly scales at base
Crownshaft: Green, smooth, long
Inflorescence: Appears below crownshaft, 4' long, branched, spreading; long season of flowering and fruiting
Gender: Separate male and female flowers on the same inflorescence
Flower Color: Greenish-white
Fruit Size: 1/2"
Fruit Color: Red
Irritant: Yes

Comments: This rainforest palm from northern Australia elicited great excitment when it was first widely introduced into the Florida nursery trade. Fast growing palms are always welcomed by nursery growers, but some of the problems associated with carpentaria have dampened this enthusiasm. The water demands of this palm are considered by some to be out of step with current trends toward water conservative landscaping. Thrips can disfigure the leaves. The palm is considerably cold tender, especially when young, and severe damage or complete loss usually follows a freeze. Despite these caveats, carpentaria is favored for its elegant form and fast growth rate. It adapts well to turf-oriented landscape irrigation, and large specimens are relatively inexpensive (except in the first year or two after a severe freeze!). It looks best when planted in closely-spaced groups of three or more. Carpentaria is reportedly short-lived, with an ultimate lifespan not much beyond 40 years. There is only one species in the genus, which is considered closely related to *Veitchia*.

Scientific Name: *Caryota mitis* (car-ē-ō-tah my-tis)
Common Name(s): Clustering fishtail palm

Typical Height: 18'
Subfamily: Arecoideae
Tribe: Caryoteae

Hardiness Zone: 10B-11
Growth Rate: Moderate
Origin: Southeast Asia

Landscape Characteristics

Salt Tolerance: Low
Drought Tolerance: Moderate
Soil Requirements: Widely adaptable
Light Requirements: Moderate, high
Nutritional Requirements: Moderate
Uses: Specimen tree
Propagation: Seeds germinating in 3-4 months
Human Hazards: Irritant
Major Pest Problems: None
Major Disease or Physiological Problems: Stigmina and other fungal leaf spots, moderate susceptibility to lethal yellowing

Morphology (Identifying Characteristics)

Habit: Clustering; stems die after fruiting; each stem with 8-10 leaves
Trunk or Stem Characteristics: Persistent long, pointed leaf bases and black fiber; eventually gray-green with widely spaced dark ring scars
Leaf Type: Bipinnately compound, induplicate; leaflets composed of about 12 secondary asymmetric, triangular leaflets irregularly toothed at tip
Foliage Color: Green
Leaf Size: 4-9' long; leaflets 4-7" long
Petiole: 2-4' long, unarmed
Crownshaft: None
Inflorescence: 1-2' long, composed of numerous pendulous branches
Gender: Separate male and female flowers on the same inflorescence
Flower Color: White
Fruit Size: 1/2"
Fruit Color: Dark red to black at maturity
Irritant: Yes

Comments: The individual stems of clustering fishtail palm cease vegetative growth after a period of years and begin to flower from the top down. After the fruit has ripened, the stem dies. Fortunately, in this species new clustering stems are continuously coming along to replace those that have fulfilled their short lease on life. The unusual form of the leaves makes this species an eye-catching specimen plant. Young plants do very well in containers as patio plants and can be acclimated to interior conditions as well. Throughout their broad native range, the fishtail palms are utilized as sources of palm sugar and starch. The fruit contains calcium oxalate crystals that are extremely irritating to the skin.

Scientific Name: *Caryota rumphiana* (car-ē-ō-tah rum-fē-**ann**-ah)
Common Name(s): Giant fishtail palm

Typical Height: 60'
Subfamily: Arecoideae
Tribe: Carytoeae

Hardiness Zone: 10B-11
Growth Rate: Fast
Origin: Southeast Asia to Australia

Landscape Characteristics

Salt Tolerance: Low
Drought Tolerance: Moderate
Soil Requirements: Widely adaptable
Light Requirements: Moderate, high
Nutritional Requirements: Moderate
Uses: Specimen tree
Propagation: Seeds, germinating in 2-3 months
Human Hazards: Irritant
Major Pest Problems: None
Major Disease or Physiological Problems:
Susceptible to lethal yellowing

Morphology (Identifying Characteristics)

Habit: Solitary; palm dies after fruiting; canopy of 10-20 leaves
Trunk or Stem Characteristics: Grayish, widely spaced rings, thickest in the middle
Leaf Type: Bipinnately compound, induplicate; leaflets somewhat pendulous
Foliage Color: Green
Leaf Size: 10-20' long
Petiole: 2-5' long; leaflets up to 15" long
Crownshaft: None
Inflorescence: 2-4' long; long, pendent branches
Gender: Separate male and female flowers on the same inflorescence
Flower Color: White
Fruit Size: 1-1.5"
Fruit Color: Purple-black
Irritant: Yes

Comments: The canopy of huge, erect, fishtail-like leaves and robust trunk of this species make it a valuable, albeit temporary specimen plant in subtropical gardens. As with all fishtail palms, the fruit should not be handled without protection from the irritating calcium oxylate crystals that they contain.

Scientific Name: *Caryota urens* (car-ē-ō-tah yū-rens)
Common Name(s): Toddy fishtail palm, Jaggery palm

Typical Height: 40'
Subfamily: Arecoideae
Tribe: Caryoteae

Hardiness Zone: 10B-11
Growth Rate: Moderate
Origin: India to Malay peninsula

Landscape Characteristics

Salt Tolerance: Low
Drought Tolerance: Moderate
Soil Requirements: Widely adaptable
Light Requirements: High
Nutritional Requirements: Moderate
Uses: Specimen tree
Propagation: Seed, germinating in 3-4 months
Human Hazards: Irritant
Major Pest Problems: None
Major Disease or Physiological Problems:
Moderately susceptible to lethal yellowing

Morphology (Identifying Characteristics)

Habit: Solitary; dies after flowering and fruiting;
canopy of 10-20 leaves
Trunk or Stem Characteristics: Gray, widely-spaced
rings, tapered towards apex
Leaf Type: Bipinnately compound, induplicate;
arching; narrow, wedge-shaped, pendulous leaflets
Foliage Color: Green
Leaf Size: 10-12' long; leaflets about 1' long
Petiole: 1-2' long, unarmed, stout
Crownshaft: None
Inflorescence: 10-14' long, pendulous, with numerous
branches
Gender: Separate male and female flowers on the same
inflorescence
Flower Color: Greenish-white
Fruit Size: 0.5" diameter
Fruit Color: Red
Irritant: Yes

Comments: This fishtail palm makes a handsome specimen plant in warm tropical areas with its crown of 10-20 ascending then arching leaves. The very large drooping inflorescences add a further ornamental dimension to the palm which increases as the red fruits appear. The flowering and fruiting process may last as long as seven years, beginning when the palm is 15-20 years old. The tree begins to die as the last fruit cluster forms in the lowest leaf axil. In its native range, the inflorescences are tapped for their sugary sap which is condensed by boiling or may be fermented into an alcoholic beverage ("toddy"). The inner pith of the stems are also a source of starch ("sagu"). Toddy palm looks its best with regular irrigation and fertilization. Young plants make attractive interiorscape subjects for bright indoor exposures. The fruits contain high levels of irritating calcium oxylate crystals and should not be handled for prolonged periods with bare hands.

Scientific Name: *Chamaedorea cataractarum* (kam-ē-**door**-ē-ah   cat-ah-rak-**tar**-um)

Common Name(s): Cat palm

Typical Height: 5'
Subfamily: Ceroxyloideae
Tribe: Hyophorbeae

Hardiness Zone: 10B-11
Growth Rate: Moderate
Origin: Southern Mexico

Landscape Characteristics

Salt Tolerance: Low
Drought Tolerance: Low, moderate in shade
Soil Requirements: Widely adaptable
Light Requirements: Moderate, low
Nutritional Requirements: Moderate
Uses: Shrub massed in beds, foliage plant
Propagation: Seed, germinating over several months
Human Hazards: Irritant
Major Pest Problems: Mealybugs, mites (indoors)
Major Disease or Physiological Problems: Gliocladium blight

Morphology (Identifying Characteristics)

Habit: Trunkless; clustering just above the base
Trunk or Stem Characteristics: Stems very short, bearing 2-6 leaves
Leaf Type: Pinnately compound, reduplicate; with numerous narrow leaflets
Foliage Color: Dark green
Leaf Size: 3-4' long; leaflets about 1' long, 3/4" wide
Petiole: Slender, unarmed, about 1' long
Crownshaft: None
Inflorescence: 1.5-2' long, yellowish-green, branched
Gender: Separate male and female plants
Flower Color: Yellow
Fruit Size: 1/4" diameter
Fruit Color: Red
Irritant: Yes

Comments: This small *Chamaedorea* species is virtually trunkless. Each stem splits just above soil level, and a beautiful, well-rounded clump is eventually formed. Cat palm is of easy culture, and is useful as a low shrubby accent in the shaded garden. It also makes an attractive potted specimen. Cat palm is more tolerant of higher light levels than many other *Chamaedorea* species, but will still bleach in sunny locations unless water and fertilizer are regularly provided.

Scientific Name: *Chamaedorea costaricana* (kam-ē-door-ē-ah kōs-tar-ē-kan-ah)
Common Name(s): Costa Rican bamboo palm

Typical Height: 10-12'
Subfamily: Ceroxyloideae
Tribe: Hyophorbeae

Hardiness Zone: 10B-11
Growth Rate: Moderate
Origin: Central America

Landscape Characteristics

Salt Tolerance: Low
Drought Tolerance: Moderate
Soil Requirements: Widely adaptable
Light Requirements: Low, moderate
Nutritional Requirements: Moderate
Uses: Specimen plant, shrub
Propagation: Seed, germinating irregularly over 1-6 months
Human Hazards: Fruit mildly irritating
Major Pest Problems: Mites, mealybugs, banana moth, scales
Major Disease or Physiological Problems: None

Morphology (Identifying Characteristics)

Habit: Densely clustering, eventually forming clumps over 6' wide; each stem with 12-24 leaves
Trunk or Stem Characteristics: Slender, smooth, green, with widely spaced ring scars
Leaf Type: Pinnately compound, reduplicate, drooping; with numerous (40 or more) narrow, thin-textured leaflets
Foliage Color: Pale green
Leaf Size: 2-4' long
Petiole: 1-2' long, unarmed
Crownshaft: None
Inflorescence: Pendulous, 2-3' long, yellowish-green in flower; female turning red in fruit
Gender: Separate male and female plants
Flower Color: Yellow
Fruit Size: 1/4" diameter
Fruit Color: Black
Irritant: Mildly

Comments: Costa Rican bamboo palm is one of strongest growers in this group of *Chamaedorea*. The species produces many stems in dense clusters which may eventually achieve a basal spread of 6' or more. It most closely resembles *C. seifrizii* but is larger and more vigorous than that species.

Scientific Name: *Chamaedorea elegans* (kam-ē-door-ē-ah eh-lah-gahnz)
Common Name(s): Parlor palm, Neanthe bella

Typical Height: 3' (but capable of reaching 6' or more)
Subfamily: Ceroxyloideae
Tribe: Hyophorbeae

Hardiness Zone: 10B-11
Growth Rate: Slow
Origin: Mexico and Central America

Landscape Characteristics

Salt Tolerance: Low
Drought Tolerance: Moderate
Soil Requirements: Widely adaptable
Light Requirements: Low, moderate
Nutritional Requirements: Moderate
Uses: Foliage plant, specimen plant
Propagation: Seed, germinating irregularly over a year; air layering
Human Hazards: Irritant
Major Pest Problems: Mites
Major Disease or Physiological Problems: Gliocladium blight, phytophthora bud rot

Morphology (Identifying Characteristics)

Habit: Solitary; canopy of 5-15 leaves
Trunk or Stem Characteristics: Slender, green, with closely spaced ring scars; aerial roots produced at stem nodes; leaves clustered near top
Leaf Type: Pinnately compound, reduplicate, deep green; leaflets lance-shaped, 20-40 regularly arranged along rachis
Foliage Color: Green
Leaf Size: 1.5-3' long; leaflets 6-9" long, about 1" wide
Petiole: 5-15" long, unarmed
Crownshaft: None
Inflorescence: .5-3' long, twice branched, orange-red, erect
Gender: Separate male and female plants
Flower color: Yellow
Fruit Size: About 1/4" diameter
Fruit Color: Black
Irritant: Yes

Comments: Parlor palm is one of the most popular indoor palms in the world, and a frequent component of dish gardens. In the outdoor landscape, it can be used as a small accent in low light, but is less conspicuous if several are planted close together. Young plants massed together can even function as a ground cover of sorts. As a houseplant, *C. elegans* will inhabit a dark corner for many months with little ill effect, but mites can be troublesome at low relative humidity. Parlor palm varies in the eventual height that individuals will reach, as well as in the size of the leaves.

Scientific Name: *Chamaedorea erumpens* (kam-ē-door-ē-ah ē-rum-pens)
Common Name(s): Bamboo palm

Typical Height: 10'
Subfamily: Ceroxyloideae
Tribe: Hyophorbeae

Hardiness Zone: 10B-11
Growth Rate: Moderate
Origin: Mexico

Landscape Characteristics

Salt Tolerance: Low
Drought Tolerance: Moderate
Soil Requirements: Widely adaptable
Light Requirements: Low, moderate
Nutritional Requirements: Moderate
Uses: Foliage plant, shrub
Propagation: Seed, germinating in 1-6 months (irregularly); division
Human Hazards: Fruit mildly irritating
Major Pest Problems: Mites, mealy bugs, banana moth
Major Disease or Physiological Problems: Gliocladium blight, phytophthora bud rot
Cultivars: 'Florida Hybrid': a hybrid between *C. seifrizii* and this species

Morphology (Identifying Characteristics)

Habit: Densely clustering, producing as many as 40 stems, each with 6-8 leaves
Trunk or Stem Characteristics: Slender, green, widely spaced rings; bamboo-like
Leaf Type: Pinnately compound, reduplicate, with about 20 leaflets, the terminal pair wider
Foliage Color: Green
Leaf Size: 18-20" long; leaflets about 8" long and 1.5" wide (terminal 3" wide)
Petiole: Short
Crownshaft: None
Inflorescence: .5-1' long, branched once, borne below the leaves, greenish in flower; female turning orange in fruit
Gender: Separate male and female plants
Flower Color: Yellow
Fruit Size: 1/4" diameter
Fruit Color: Black
Irritant: Mildly

Comments: *Chamaedorea erumpens* is similar in most respects to *C. seifrizii*, except for its wider leaflets, and some authorities consider it only a variety of that species. Like that species, it can be used effectively as an understory shrub in the tropical garden, a low screening plant in shady areas, or as an indoor foliage plant.

Scientific Name: *Chamaedorea metallica* (kam-ē-**door**-ē-ah   met-**tal**-eh-kah)
Common Name(s): Miniature fishtail palm

Typical Height: 4'
Subfamily: Ceroxyloideae
Tribe: Hyophorbeae

Hardiness Zone: 10B-11
Growth Rate: Slow
Origin: Mexico

Landscape Characteristics

Salt Tolerance: Low
Drought Tolerance: Moderate
Soil Requirements: Widely adaptable
Light Requirements: Low, moderate
Nutritional Requirements: Moderate
Uses: Specimen plant massed in beds, foliage plant
Propagation: Seed, germinating in several months
Human Hazards: Mild irritant
Major Pest Problems: Mealybugs, scales
Major Disease or Physiological Problems: None

Morphology (Identifying Characteristics)

Habit: Solitary; canopy of 10-15 leaves
Trunk or Stem Characteristics: Slender, dark green; ring scars closely spaced; aerial roots near base; leaves clustered near top
Leaf Type: Simple, two-lobed, reduplicate; slightly toothed on upper margins; puckered on surface; occasionally pinnately compound
Foliage Color: Metallic blue-green
Leaf Size: 10-12" long, 5-8" wide
Petiole: Short, slender, 4-6" long
Crownshaft: None
Inflorescence: Erect; the male branched, 1-1.5' long; the female a spike
Gender: Separate male and female plants
Flower Color: Cream
Fruit Size: About 1/2" long
Fruit Color: Black
Irritant: Mildly

Comments: This fishtail-leafed *Chamaedorea* is unique in the genus for the beautiful, shiny blue-green cast of its broad and (usually) two-lobed leaves. It is most striking when several plants are placed close together, whether in the landscape or in containers. The leaves look their best if the plant is protected from drying winds and strong sunlight. This species prospers in soils with increased amounts of organic material. On sandy soils, regular application of mulch is beneficial. *C. metallica* makes an excellent indoor plant as well, and will occupy a dark corner for months in good condition.

Similar Species: *C. ernesti-augusti* is an allied species similar in appearance to *C. metallica* but lacking the distinctive metallic sheen and color. It produces aerial roots at nodes along the entire stem like *C. elegans*, and can reach over 6' in height.

Scientific Name: *Chamaedorea microspadix* (kam-ē-door-ē-ah my-kro-spā-diks)
Common Name(s): Hardy bamboo palm

Typical Height: 8'
Subfamily: Ceroxyloideae
Tribe: Hyophorbeae

Hardiness Zone: 9-11
Growth Rate: Moderate
Origin: Mexico

Landscape Characteristics

Salt Tolerance: Low
Drought Tolerance: Moderate
Soil Requirements: Widely adaptable
Light Requirements: Low, moderate
Nutritional Requirements: Moderate
Uses: Shrub, specimen plant, screen
Propagation: Seed, germinating over several months
Human Hazards: Irritant
Major Pest Problems: Mealybugs
Major Disease or Physiological Problems: None

Morphology (Identifying Characteristics)

Habit: Clustering, stems sometimes widely separated, each bearing 4-8 leaves
Trunk or Stem Characteristics: Slender, green, with prominent, moderately wide-spaced ring scars; leaves persist on lower portions of stems
Leaf Type: Pinnately compound, reduplicate, with only 16-20 broad, thin, regularly arranged leaflets
Foliage Color: Dull green
Leaf Size: 15-24" long; leaflets 6-10" long, 1-2" wide
Petiole: Short, slender, unarmed
Crownshaft: None
Inflorescence: 1-2' long, branched once, drooping, yellowish-green; borne below the leaves
Gender: Separate male and female plants
Flower Color: Cream
Fruit Size: About 1/4" diameter
Fruit Color: Orange-red
Irritant: Yes

Comments: Hardy bamboo palm, like *C. radicalis*, extends the outdoor utility of the genus *Chamaedorea* to areas where freezing temperatures are experienced in the winter. With some protection, plants have withstood temperatures below 20° F with little or no damage. Certainly the hardiest reed-stem *Chamaedorea* currently enjoying wide cultivation, *C. microspadix* superficially resembles the tender bamboo palms such as *C. seifrizii* and *C. erumpens*, but can be distinguished by the distance often observed between stems in the cluster and the its fewer leaflets. Hardy bamboo palm makes a fine specimen plant in part shade, and can also be used as coarse screening plant. It is equally at home in the interior, and is one of the more mite resistant species of *Chamaedorea*.

Scientific Name: *Chamaedorea radicalis* (kam-ē-door-ē-ah rad-eh-**kal**-is)

Common Name(s): Radicalis palm

Typical Height: 5' (but capable of reaching 10')
Subfamily: Ceroxyloideae
Tribe: Hyophorbeae

Hardiness Zone: 9-11
Growth Rate: Slow
Origin: Mexico

Landscape Characteristics

Salt Tolerance: Low
Drought Tolerance: Moderate
Soil Requirements: Widely adaptable
Light Requirements: Low, moderate
Nutritional Requirements: Moderate
Uses: Shrub, foliage plant
Propagation: Seed, germinating over several months
Human Hazards: Fruit mildly irritating
Major Pest Problems: None
Major Disease or Physiological Problems: None

Morphology (Identifying Characteristics)

Habit: Often trunkless, clustering from the base; each stem with 6-8 leaves
Trunk or Stem Characteristics: Short, slender
Leaf Type: Pinnately compound, reduplicate, with several dozen narrow leaflets
Foliage Color: Dark green
Leaf Size: About 3' long; leaflets about 1' long, 1" wide
Petiole: Short, unarmed
Crownshaft: None
Infloresence: About 4' long, held above the leaves, branched once, greenish in flower; female turns orange in fruit
Gender: Separate male and female plants
Flower Color: Yellow-orange
Fruit Size: Slighty less than 1/2" diameter
Fruit Color: Orange
Irritant: Mildly

Comments: This frequently stemless *Chamaedorea* is becoming more widely available and is as hardy as *C. microspadix*. It prospers in warm, shady sites in the landscape. Somewhat more open in growth than cat palm, it can be used similarly as an understory shrub in combination with other tropicals. It reportedly performs well in the interior. It begins to flower when quite young.

Scientific Name: *Chamaedorea seifrizii* (kam-ē-door-ē-ah sē-friz-ē-ī)

Common Name(s): Bamboo palm, Reed palm

Typical Height: 7' (but can achieve 12')
Subfamily: Ceroxyloideae
Tribe: Hyophorbeae

Hardiness Zone: 10B-11
Growth Rate: Moderate
Origin: Mexico and northern Central America

Landscape Characteristics

Salt Tolerance: Low
Drought Tolerance: Moderate
Soil Requirements: Widely adaptable
Light Requirements: Low, moderate
Nutritional Requirements: Moderate
Uses: Shrub, screen, specimen plant, foliage plant
Propagation: Seed, germinating over 6 or more months
Human Hazards: Irritant
Major Pest Problems: Mites, mealy bugs, scales
Major Disease or Physiological Problems: Gliocladium blight, phytophthora bud rot
Cultivars: 'Florida Hybrid': a hybrid between *C. seifrizii* and *C. erumpens*

Morphology (Identifying Characteristics)

Habit: Clustering densely; each stem bearing 6-9 leaves
Trunk or Stem Characteristics: Upright, slender, dark green with widely spaced and conspicuous ring scars
Leaf Type: Pinnately compound, reduplicate; 2-3 dozen narrow leaflets crowded on the stem
Foliage Color: Dull, medium green
Leaf Size: About 2' long; leaflets 8" long, .5-.75" wide
Petiole: Short, unarmed
Crownshaft: None
Inflorescence: Short, .5-1' long, branched once, males greenish, females turning orange in fruit; borne below the leaves
Gender: Separate male and female plants
Flower Color: Yellow
Fruit Size: 1/4" diameter
Fruit Color: Black
Irritant: Yes

Comments: One of the most popular *Chamaedorea* species, *C. seifrizii* has less coarser foliage than *C. erumpens* which it somewhat resembles. It eventually forms fairly dense clumps of very erect stems with an overall aspect of bamboo. The canopy of leaves is open, and concentrated in the upper half of the stem. Reed palm is moderately sun-tolerant, but is most at home in shady locations. Most nurseries grow this palm in full sun for the first year or two of production to stimulate cluster development before moving them under shade. It is also tolerant of less fertile soils than many other *Chamaedorea* species.

Scientific Name: *Chamaedorea tepejilote* (kam-ē-door-ē-ah tā-pā-hē-lō-tā)

Common Name(s): Pacaya

Typical Height: 10'
Subfamily: Ceroxyloideae
Tribe: Hyophorbeae

Hardiness Zone: 10B-11
Growth Rate: Fast
Origin: Mexico to Colombia

Landscape Characteristics

Salt Tolerance: Low
Drought Tolerance: Moderate
Soil Requirements: Widely adaptable
Light Requirements: Moderate, low
Nutritional Requirements: Moderate
Uses: Specimen plant, shrub, foliage plant
Propagation: Seed, germinating in several months; air-layering
Human Hazards: Irritant
Major Pest Problems: Mites, scales, mealybugs
Major Disease or Physiological Problems: Gliocladium blight
Cultivars: A variable species with many regional cultivars in Central America selected on the basis of the quality of the edible male inflorescences (known as pacaya or pacayaita) which are highly prized, especially in Guatemala

Morphology (Identifying Characteristics)

Habit: Usually solitary (often offered as mutiples by nurseries) but sometimes clustering; bears 5-7 leaves
Trunk or Stem Characteristics: Slender, green, conspicuously ringed, producing aerial roots
Leaf Type: Pinnately compound, reduplicate, with 3-4 dozen ribbed leaflets that fall from the stem with age
Foliage Color: Dark green
Leaf Size: To 5' long; leaflets 18-24" long, 1.5-2" wide
Petiole: Short, about 18" long, unarmed
Crownshaft: Short, green
Inflorescence: To 2' long, borne below the crown, shortly once-branched, yellowish-green; females are longer, thicker than males, and turn orange in fruit
Gender: Separate male and female plants
Flower Color: Yellow
Fruit Size: 1/2" diameter
Fruit Color: Black
Irritant: Yes

Comments: The male inflorescences of this solitary *Chamaedorea* species are a prized market commodity in Guatemala and other parts of Central America. They are pickled, or sliced fresh and used in soups, omelettes and other dishes. Pacaya is much faster growing than many of the more popular *Chamaedorea* species, and is becoming more widely available for this reason. Solitary forms are often planted as a multiple specimen, and in this fashion can be mistaken for one of the bamboo or reed palms. Like most members of the genus, it favors a shaded spot in the tropical garden, and is useful as a specimen or accent in close quarters where larger palms might be outsized.

Scientific Name: *Chamaerops humilis* (kam-ē-rops hū-mil-is)
Common Name(s): European fan palm

Typical Height: 10'
Subfamily: Coryphoideae
Tribe: Corypheae

Hardiness Zone: 8-11
Growth Rate: Slow
Origin: Mediterranean region

Landscape Characteristics

Salt Tolerance: Moderate (possibly high for natively coastal forms)
Drought Tolerance: High (once well-established)
Soil Requirements: Widely adaptable
Light Requirements: High, moderate
Nutritional Requirements: Moderate
Uses: Specimen plant, shrub, container plant
Propagation: Seeds, germinating in 2-3 months; possibly division
Human Hazards: Spiny
Major Pest Problems: Scales, palm aphid, ambrosia beetle
Major Disease or Physiological Problems: Potassium deficiency (Florida), ganoderma, fungal leaf spots
Cultivars: Many forms occur throughout the range of this species, some of which have been named in the past

Morphology (Identifying Characteristics)

Habit: Usually clustering, but solitary forms occur; canopy of 15-30 leaves
Trunk or Stem Characteristics: About 1' diameter; dead leaves persist below crown; covered for many years with dense, brown fibers
Leaf Type: Palmate, very deeply divided into several dozen narrow segments which split at their tips
Foliage Color: Green, blue-green or silvery green; glossy or dull
Leaf Size: About 3' in diameter
Petiole: 3-5' long; armed with fierce orange teeth that point toward leaf
Crownshaft: None
Inflorescence: Short, about 6" long, with thick branches, hidden among the leaves
Gender: Usually separate male and female plants
Flower Color: Yellow
Fruit Size: About 1/2" diameter
Fruit Color: Yellow, orange or brown
Irritant: No

Comments: This hardy fan palm occurs throughout the Mediterranean region, from coastal zones to over 3000' in elevation, and in various types of vegetation. In mountain habitats, it has been known to even receive snow cover. Throughout this broad range, it is typically found on poor, rocky soils, and thus is very adaptable to a wide range of soil types in the landscape as long as they are well-drained. It is highly prized in warm temperate areas where few palms are reliably winter hardy, and a large clump makes a striking specimen plant. The skirt of dead leaves below the crown is usually trimmed off to accent the mat of dark fibers that clothe the trunk for many years. The variation in leaf color and habit is extraordinary. In a nursery row of European fan palms, it is sometimes difficult to find any two that look exactly alike. Its slow rate of growth allows this palm to be grown in a large container for many years. Growth of *C. humilis* is best in full sun, but it also retains an excellent appearance in light shade.

Scientific Name: *Chrysalidocarpus cabadae* (cry-sal-id-o-car-pus kah-**bah**-dē)

Common Name(s): Cabada palm

Typical Height: 30'
Subfamily: Arecoideae
Tribe: Areceae

Hardiness Zone: 10B-11
Growth Rate: Moderate
Origin: Probably Madagascar (known only from cultivation)

Landscape Characteristics

Salt Tolerance: Moderate
Drought Tolerance: High
Soil Requirements: Widely adaptable
Light Requirements: Moderate, high
Nutritional Requirements: Moderate
Uses: Multi-trunked specimen tree, large shrub
Propagation: Seed, germinating in 1-2 months
Human Hazards: None
Major Pest Problems: None
Major Disease or Physiological Problems: Slightly susceptible to lethal yellowing, stigmina leaf spot, potassium deficiency, ganoderma

Morphology (Identifying Characteristics)

Habit: Clustering, each stem with 6-10 leaves
Trunk or Stem Characteristics: Smooth, bright green, prominently ringed with grayish-white leaf scars
Leaf Type: Pinnately compound, reduplicate; numerous leaflets in one plane; arching near the tip
    Foliage Color: Medium green
    Leaf Size: 8-10'; leaflets approximately 2' long, 2" wide
    Petiole: Short, 1-2' long, unarmed
    Crownshaft: Greenish-gray
    Inflorescence: To 5' long, branched, appearing below the crownshaft
    Gender: Separate male and female flowers on the same inflorescence
    Flower Color: Yellow
    Fruit Size: 1/2"
    Fruit Color: Red
    Irritant: No

Comments: This elegant clustering palm grows larger and more slowly than its relative, the areca (*C. lutescens*). The Cabada palm makes a striking architectural accent in the landscape, with its smooth, boldly ringed green trunks. The Cabada palm may be slow to cluster; several specimens can be planted close together to create a fuller effect. Young plants frequently have reddish-brown petioles and leaf sheaths; this fades with age. The cabada palm is very effective in courtyard settings or other close spaces where its eye-catching trunk can be shown to advantage. Presumed to have originated in Madagascar, the Cabada palm was discovered in a Cuban garden.

Scientific Name: *Chrysalidocarpus lucubensis* (cry-sal-id-ō-car-pus loo-kū-ben-sis)
Common Name(s): Lucubensis palm

Typical Height: 30'
Subfamily: Arecoideae
Tribe: Areceae

Hardiness Zone: 10B-11
Growth Rate: Moderate
Origin: Nossi Be Island (off Madagascar)

Landscape Characteristics

Salt Tolerance: Moderate
Drought Tolerance: Moderate
Soil Requirements: Widely adaptable
Light Requirements: Moderate, high
Nutritional Requirements: Moderate
Uses: Specimen tree
Propagation: Seed, germinating in 2-5 months
Human Hazards: None
Major Pest Problems: None
Major Disease or Physiological Problems: Potassium deficiency (Florida)

Morphology (Identifying Characteristics)

Habit: Solitary; canopy of 9-12 leaves arranged in 3 vertical rows
Trunk or Stem Characteristics: Green for many years, eventually gray, prominently ringed with raised leaf scars
Leaf Type: Pinnately compound, reduplicate; with over 200 slightly drooping leaflets in variously ranked groups of 3-4 giving the leaf a plume-like appearance
Foliage Color: Deep green
Leaf Size: 10' long; leaflets 1.5-2' long, 1" wide
Petiole: 1/2' long or less, unarmed
Crownshaft: Short, bright green, waxy white near top
Inflorescence: 2-4' long, densely branched
Gender: Separate male and female flowers on the same inflorescence
Flower Color: Yellow
Fruit Size: 1/2" long
Fruit Color: Black
Irritant: No

Comments: This beautiful relative of the areca palm is starting to become more widely available. The crown, though sparse in leaf number, has an attractive tiered arrangement augmented by the full, plume-like character of the leaves.

Similar Species: *C. madagascariensis* (Madagscar) is very similar in appearance except that it clusters with 2-6 stems. Lucubensis palm is sometimes treated as a variety of this species.

Scientific Name: *Chrysalidocarpus lutescens* (cry-sal-id-ō-**car**-pus loo-**tess**-sens)
Common Name(s): Areca palm, Butterfly palm

Typical Height: 20'
Subfamily: Arecoideae
Tribe: Areceae

Hardiness Zone: 10B-11
Growth Rate: Moderate
Origin: Madagascar

Comments: The areca palm is so widely planted throughout sub-tropical and tropical climates, it is often treated with contempt by palm enthusiasts. Despite its ubiquity in cultivation, the species is much rarer in its native Madagascar. Though most often thickly planted as a screen or boundary hedge, areca palm can make an attractive specimen plant in time when a measure of clear trunk is achieved, and the cluster is opened up by judicious thinning out of some stems. Unfortunately, containerized specimens are usually produced by potting numerous seedlings together which, when planted in the landscape, form dense and frequently stunted clusters. On soils with low fertility, the foliage is usually marred with nutritional deficiencies, but, with regular fertilization, the leaflets will hold a medium green coloration that contrasts nicely with the naturally yellow-tinged leafstems. Arecas are also widely produced for the foliage plant market, but suffer in dim light and low humidity.

Scientific Name: *Coccothrinax alta* (kō-kō-thrī-naks all-tah)

Common Name(s): Silver palm

Typical Height: 25'
Subfamily: Coryphoideae
Tribe: Corypheae

Hardiness Zone: 10B-11
Growth Rate: Slow
Origin: Puerto Rico and Virgin Islands

Landscape Characteristics

Salt Tolerance: High
Drought Tolerance: High
Soil Requirements: Widely adaptable
Light Requirements: Moderate, high
Nutritional Requirements: Low
Uses: Small specimen tree, seaside landscapes
Propagation: Seed, germinating in 3 months or more, best at high temperature
Human Hazards: None
Major Pest Problems: None
Major Disease or Physiological Problems: None

Morphology (Identifying Characteristics)

Habit: Solitary; canopy of 12-15 leaves
Trunk or Stem Characteristics: Slender, light gray-brown, slightly ringed, upper portion matted with brown leaf base fibers
Leaf Type: Palmate, induplicate, nearly circular, divided 1/2 to 2/3 into broad, 2- lobed segments
Foliage Color: Green above, silvery below
Leaf Size: About 3' in diameter; segments 2" wide
Petiole: About 3' long, unarmed
Crownshaft: None
Inflorescence: 1-2' long, branched
Gender: Flowers bisexual
Flower Color: White
Fruit Size: 3/8" diameter
Fruit Color: Shiny brown to black
Irritant: No

Comments: This slow-growing silver palm attains larger size and spread than the Florida native *C. argentata*. Like most *Coccothrinax* species, it is very tolerant of dry, alkaline soils and coastal exposures.

Scientific Name: *Coccothrinax argentata* (kō-kō-**thrī**-naks ar-gen-**tah**-tah)
Common Name(s): Silver palm

Typical Height: 15' (but frequently smaller)
Subfamily: Coryphoideae
Tribe: Corypheae

Hardiness Zone: l0B-11
Growth Rate: Slow
Origin: Florida and the Bahamas

Landscape Characteristics

Salt Tolerance: High
Drought Tolerance: High
Soil Requirements: Widely adaptable
Light Requirements: Moderate, high
Nutritional Requirements: Low
Uses: Small specimen tree, seaside locations
Propagation: Seed, germinating in 3-6 months with heat
Human Hazards: None
Major Pest Problems: None
Major Disease or Physiological Problems:
Phytophthora bud rot if over-watered, graphiola false smut

Morphology (Identifying Characteristics)

Habit: Solitary
Trunk or Stem Characteristics: Slender, smooth, light gray, indistinctly ringed, matted with fiber in upper regions; bearing about 16 leaves
Leaf Type: Palmate, induplicate, divided to about 3/4 into 40+ segments which are split at their tip and droop
Foliage Color: Green above, densely silver below
Leaf Size: About 3' diameter; segments 1" wide
Petiole: About 2.5' long, unarmed
Crownshaft: None
Infloresence: 2' long, with short branches
Gender: Bisexual flowers
Flower Color: White, fragrant
Fruit Size: 1/2" diameter
Fruit Color: Black
Irritant: No

Comments: Florida's native silver palm can sometimes be found growing with its roots wedged within cracks on limestone outcrops, its trunks blackened by pineland fires. As this suggests, it is an extemely tough and durable palm, with an intensely silver underside to the leaves that seems to glint in the sun.

Other Species: *C. argentea*. This species, native to Hispaniola, is larger in all respect than *C. argentata*, with more rigid leaves that are less silvery on the underside.

Scientific Name: *Coccothrinax crinita* (kō-kō-thrī-naks krin-ē-tah)
Common Name(s): Old man palm

Typical Height: 15'
Subfamily: Coryphoideae
Tribe: Corypheae

Hardiness Zone: 10B-11
Growth Rate: Slow
Origin: Cuba

Landscape Characteristics

Salt Tolerance: High
Drought Tolerance: Moderate
Soil Requirements: Widely adaptable
Light Requirements: Moderate, high
Nutritional Requirements: Low
Uses: Small specimen tree, container plant
Propagation: Seed, germinating in six months
Human Hazards: None
Major Pest Problems: Nematodes if drought stressed
Major Disease or Physiological Problems:
Phytophthora bud rot if over-watered

Morphology (Identifying Characteristics)

Habit: Solitary; 15-25 leaves
Trunk or Stem Characteristics: Slender, densely
covered with long, straw-colored hair-like fiber that
makes the trunk look thicker
Leaf Type: Palmate, induplicate, almost circular, rigid,
divided more than 3/4 into 30 or more segments that are
split at their tips
Foliage Color: Dark green above, grayish below
Leaf Size: To 5' in diameter; segments about 2" wide
Petiole: 4' long, unarmed
Crownshaft: None
Inflorescence: 5' long, branched
Gender: Bisexual flowers
Flower Color: Yellow
Fruit Size: 1" long
Fruit Color: Purple
Irritant: No

Comments: This delightful fan palm is remarkable for the long shag of hair that
clothes the stem, even when the plant is young. It is very slow-growing, however, and
large specimens fetch a handsome price. Old man palm is no more demanding than
other members of the same genus, and adapts well to alkaline soils and coastal exposures. It is native to seasonally flooded savanna in Cuba.

Scientific Name: *Coccothrinax miraguama* (kō-kō-thrī-naks mer-ah-**gua**-mah)
Common Name(s): Miraguama palm

Typical Height: 20'
Subfamily: Coryphoideae
Tribe: Corypheae

Hardiness Zone: 10B-11
Growth Rate: Moderate
Origin: Cuba

Landscape Characteristics

Salt Tolerance: High
Drought Tolerance: High
Soil Requirements: Widely adaptable
Light Requirements: Moderate, high
Nutritional Requirements: Low
Uses: Small tree
Propagation: Seed, germinating in 2-3 months
Human Hazards: None
Major Pest Problems: None
Major Disease or Physiological Problems: Potassium deficiency (Florida)
Cultivars: Several regional varieties have been described by botanists

Morphology (Identifying Characteristics)

Habit: Solitary; canopy of 20-30 leaves
Trunk or Stem Characteristics: Variable, smooth and gray with indistinct ring scars or covered with matted fiber and protruding leaf bases
Leaf Type: Palmate, induplicate, circular, stiff; divided halfway or more into 40-60 pointed segments that abruptly taper inward near the tip
Foliage Color: Dark green above, silvery below
Leaf Size: 2-5' wide; segments 2' long, 2" wide
Petiole: 3-4' long, thin, unarmed
Crownshaft: None
Inflorescence: 3' long, branched, borne from among the leaves
Gender: Bisexual flowers
Flower Color: Yellowish-white
Fruit Size: 1/2" diameter
Fruit Color: Red ripening to black or purple
Irritant: No

Comments: Miraguama palm is one of the most attractive species in the genus, with a faster than average growth rate. The leaves form neat circles giving the canopy a more formal appearance than most *Coccothrinax* species. Miraguama palm makes a fine showing in group plantings. Individuals can vary as to the degree of matting on the trunk as well as in trunk thickness and height.

Scientific Name: *Cocos nucifera* (kō-kōs new-sif-er-ah)
Common Name(s): Coconut palm

Typical Height: 50-80'
Subfamily: Arecoideae
Tribe: Cocoeae

Hardiness Zone: 10B-11
Growth Rate: Moderate
Origin: Probably the Pacific Islands, but now distributed world-wide in tropics

Landscape Characteristics

Salt Tolerance: High
Drought Tolerance: High
Soil Requirements: Widely adaptable
Light Requirements: High
Nutritional Requirements: Moderate
Uses: Shade tree, specimen tree, edible fruit, commercial source of oil & fiber
Propagation: Seed, germinating in 4-6 months
Human Hazards: None
Major Pest Problems: Palm aphid, coconut mite, red ring nematode (outside U.S.)
Major Disease or Physiological Problems: Susceptible to lethal yellowing (varies with cultivar); potassium deficiency, phytophthora bud rot, ganoderma
Cultivars: 'Jamaican Tall' and 'Panama Tall': very susceptible to LY. 'Malayan Dwarf': green and golden forms, slender trunk, begins flowering when young, greens more susceptible to LY than goldens. 'Maypan': hybrid of 'Panama Tall' and golden 'Malayan Dwarf', resistant to LY. Many others

Morphology (Identifying Characteristics)

Habit: Solitary, very rarely producing a sucker or two, bearing 20-30 leaves
Trunk or Stem Characteristics: Sometimes curved, base often swollen, grayish- brown, with conspicuous, cresent-shaped leaf scars; fiber matting above
Leaf Type: Pinnately compound, reduplicate, slightly twisted, eventually drooping, with 150-200 leaflets
Foliage Color: Dark to light green or yellowish-green
Leaf Size: 15 or more feet long; leaflets 3' long, 1.5" wide
Petiole: 3-4' long, unarmed
Crownshaft: None
Inflorescence: 3-5' long, thick, few-branched or spike-like; surrounded at base by a persistant, conspicuous bract
Gender: Separate male and female flowers on the same inflorescence
Flower Color: White
Fruit Size: 1' long
Fruit Color: Green, yellow, orange; eventually brown
Irritant: No

Comments: Coconut palms are the universal symbol of the tropics, and inarguably the world's most economically important palm. Copra (the dried "meat" of the seed), from which oil is extracted, is a significant cash crop throughout the tropics. Coir, the fiber from the fruit husk, is widely used in manufacturing. The fruits yield several food products at different stages of development, and the leaves are used for thatch or are woven into baskets, mats, and clothing. Even the trunks have been utilized for construction. The trees are valued for their ability to adapt to exposed coastal locations, prospering best in areas with high rainfall, high water tables (though long-term flooding is not tolerated), and warm temperatures. In frost-free but cool climates, the palms grow more slowly and may not flower. Lethal yellowing is the most serious problem of coconuts. The disease is presently incurable, and is spread by a tropical leaf hopper bug. A program of antibiotic injections will temporarily suspend the decline of infected palms while resistant replacements are being established nearby.

Scientific Name: *Copernicia baileyana* (kō-per-nē-sē-ah bā-lē-**ann**-ah)
Common Name(s): Bailey copernicia

Typical Height: 40'
Subfamily: Coryphoideae
Tribe: Corypheae

Hardiness Zone: 10B-11
Growth Rate: Slow
Origin: Cuba

Older.

Younger.

Youngest.

Landscape Characteristics

Salt Tolerance: Moderate
Drought Tolerance: High
Soil Requirements: Widely adaptable
Light Requirements: High
Nutritional Requirements: Low
Uses: Specimen tree
Propagation: Seed, germinating in 1-3 months
Human Hazards: Spiny
Major Pest Problems: None
Major Disease or Physiological Problems: None

Morphology (Identifying Characteristics)

Habit: Solitary, bearing 50 or more leaves
Trunk or Stem Characteristics: Smooth, gray, massive (to 5' wide), leaf scars inconspicuous; broad leaf bases persisting on upper portions
Leaf Type: Costapalmate, induplicate, divided about 1/3 into over a hundred stiff segments that split at their tips
Foliage Color: Green
Leaf Size: 5' diameter; segments 2" wide
Petiole: 4-5' long, broad, armed with coarse teeth
Crownshaft: None
Inflorescence: 5-7' long, much-branched, produced from among and extending past leaves
Gender: Bisexual flowers
Flower Color: Cream
Fruit Size: 3/4" diameter
Fruit Color: Dark brown
Irritant: No

Comments: This Cuban relative of the carnauba wax palm is highly regarded for the imposing girth of its trunk, topped by a dense crown of beautiful, rigid leaves. It requires ample room, is slow to establish, but is arguably one of the most magnificant fan palms in the world. The *Copernicia* palms as a group consist of about two dozen species, the majority of which are native to Cuba.

Scientific Name: *Copernicia hospita* (kō-per-nē-sē-ah hos-pit-ah)

Common Name(s): Hospita palm

Typical Height: 30' (but can reach 50')
Subfamily: Coryphoideae
Tribe: Corypheae

Hardiness Zone: 10B-11
Growth Rate: Slow
Origin: Cuba

Landscape Characteristics

Salt Tolerance: Moderate
Drought Tolerance: High
Soil Requirements: Widely adaptable
Light Requirements: High
Nutritional Requirements: Low
Uses: Specimen tree
Propagation: Seeds, germinating in 1-3 months
Human Hazards: Spiny
Major Pest Problems: None
Major Disease or Physiological Problems: None

Morphology (Identifying Characteristics)

Habit: Solitary; canopy of 20-30 leaves
Trunk or Stem Characteristics: Gray, indistinctly ringed; dead leaves form skirt below the crown
Leaf Type: Costapalmate, induplicate, wedge-shaped with wide costa and long hastula; divided about 1/3 into 18-30 segments; margins toothed
Foliage Color: Blue-green to green, waxy
Leaf Size: 5-7' long, 2' wide; segments 2" wide
Petiole: None (the leaves appear to rise directly from the trunk)
Crownshaft: None
Inflorescence: About 6' long, slender, branched, extending out from the leaves
Gender: Bisexual flowers
Flower Color: Brown
Fruit Size: About 3/8" diameter
Fruit Color: Green
Irritant: No

Comments: Hospita palm is one of the striking *Copernicia* species that lack a substantial leaf stem ("sessile" in botanical parlance). The unusually narrow leaves seem to rise directly from the trunk, and form an erect crown on mature trees of impressive dimensions and appearance. The shallow segments of the leaf are rigid at first, but later drooping. The leaves are further marked distinctively by the long, broad leaf stem extension (costa) that penetrates several feet into the leaf blade and an often equally long hastula on the upper surface which juts out from the blade. The leaves are also spiny margined, and small teeth are also found on some of the ribs within the blade. This Cuban species is well-adapted to seasonally dry, warm tropical areas, though its slow rate of growth keeps it uncommon. "Young" specimens (without much trunk development) are supremely distinctive looking.

Similar Species: *C. rigida* (jata palm), also from Cuba, is very similar to the hospita palm, but bears only green leaves.

Scientific Name: *Copernicia macroglossa* (kō-per-nē-sē-ah   mak-rō-**gloss**-ah)

Common Name(s): Cuban petticoat palm

Typical Height: 15'
Subfamily: Coryphoideae
Tribe: Corypheae

Hardiness Zone: 10B-11
Growth Rate: Slow
Origin: Cuba

Landscape Characteristics

Salt Tolerance: Moderate
Drought Tolerance: High
Soil Requirements: Widely adaptable
Light Requirements: High
Nutritional Requirements: Low
Uses: Specimen tree
Propagation: Seed, germinating in 1-3 months
Human Hazards: Spiny
Major Pest Problems: None
Major Disease or Physiological Problems: None

Morphology (Identifying Characteristics)

Habit: Solitary; canopy of 12-15 leaves
Trunk or Stem characteristics: Gray, slender, but clothed to base for many years with a skirt of dead leaves (unless these are trimmed)
Leaf Type: Costapalmate, induplicate, broadly wedge-shaped, with teeth scattered along margin; divided about 1/3 into sixty segments
Foliage Color: Light green, waxy
Leaf Size: 5-7' wide
Petiole: Absent to very short (1 foot or less)
Crownshaft: None
Inflorescence: About 6' long, slender, branched, extending beyond the leaves
Gender: Bisexual flowers
Flower Color: Brown
Fruit Size: 3/4" diameter
Fruit Color: Green
Irritant: No

Comments: The trunk of Cuban petticoat palm, when fully "shagged" with dead leaves, appears deceptively massive; below the thatch of its petticoat, the actual trunk is no more than 8" thick. Like *C. hospita*, the leaves of this species lack a well-developed leaf stem (petiole), but are broader and with a less conspicuous leaf stem extension into the blade. The hastula is quite long. Typically, the canopy of Cuban petticoat palm consists of about a dozen erect green leaves. The leaves droop as they age and will persist for many years unless removed.

Scientific Name: *Copernicia prunifera* (ko-per-ne-se-ah pru-nif-ir-ah)
Common Name(s): Carnauba wax palm

Typical Height: 30'
Subfamily: Coryphoideae
Tribe: Corypheae

Hardiness Zone: 10B-11
Growth Rate: Slow to moderate
Origin: Brazil

Landscape Characteristics

Salt Tolerance: Moderate
Drought Tolerance: Moderate
Soil Requirements: Widely adaptable
Light Requirements: High
Nutritional Requirements: Low
Uses: Specimen tree; leaf wax is commercial product in Brazil
Propagation: Seed, germinating in 1-3 months
Human Hazards: Spiny
Major Pest Problems: None
Major Disease or Physiological Problems: None

Morphology (Identifying Characteristics)

Habit: Solitary; canopy of about 2 dozen leaves
Trunk or Stem Characteristics: Gray, smooth, leaf scars only partially circle trunk; leaf bases oddly persist on lower trunk
Leaf Type: Palmate, induplicate; divided more than halfway into 30-60 narrow segments that barely split at their tips
Foliage Color: Blue-green, very waxy
Leaf Size: 3.5' wide, segments 1/2" wide
Petiole: 2.5-3' long; armed throughout length with large, curved black teeth
Crownshaft: None
Inflorescence: 5-7' long, slender, branched
Gender: Bisexual flowers
Flower Color: Brown
Fruit Size: 1" long
Fruit Color: Brown
Irritant: No

Comments: One of three *Copernicia* species that occur in South America, the carnauba wax palm is valued in Brazil for the copious quantity of heat resistant wax found on its leaves. Leaves are harvested, dried, and the wax beaten from them for processing into various waxes and polishes. In its native habitat, the carnauba wax palm is subject to flooding, and thus may have landscape tolerance for less well-drained sites than Cuban *Copernicia* species. The carnauba wax palm is also slightly faster growing than its West Indian cousins. The leaf bases of carnauba wax palms curiously persist on the lower 1/3 of the trunk while falling cleanly from the upper portions. While not as drought tolerant or dramatic in appearance as the sessile-leafed *Copernicia* species (those lacking leaf stems), carnauba wax palm makes an attractive specimen tree in tropical gardens.

Similar Species: *C. alba*, the carnaday palm, occurs in Paraguay, northern Argentina, Bolivia, and contiguous southwestern Brazil. It often forms enormous populations. Resembling the carnauba wax palm in most respects, it is also a secondary commercial source of industrial grade wax.

Scientific Name: *Corypha utan* (kō-rye-fah oo-tahn)
Common Name(s): Gebang palm

Typical Height: 60'
Subfamily: Coryphoideae
Tribe: Corypheae

Hardiness Zone: 10B-11
Growth Rate: Moderate (slow when young)
Origin: Southeast Asia, East Indies, Australia

Talipot palm in fruit.

Young gebang palm.

Landscape Characteristics

Salt Tolerance: Low
Drought Tolerance: High
Soil Requirements: Widely adaptable
Light Requirements: High
Nutritional Requirements: Moderate
Uses: Specimen tree
Propagation: Seeds, germinating in 2-3 months (best if fresh)
Human Hazards: Spiny
Major Pest Problems: None
Major Disease or Physiological Problems: Moderate susceptibility to lethal yellowing

Morphology (Identifying Characteristics)

Habit: Solitary; flowers, fruits, then dies; canopy of about 3 dozen leaves
Trunk or Stem Characteristics: Gray, robust, leaf bases persist when young; ringed with spiraled, swollen leaf scars
Leaf Type: Costapalmate, induplicate, round, divided to about 1/2 into 80-100 tapering segments that are split at their tips
Foliage Color: Light green
Leaf Size: 12-18' in diameter; segments 6.5' long, 2.5" wide
Petiole: 6-12' long, thick, gray to yellow, black teeth on margins, base split
Crownshaft: None
Inflorescence: Appearing terminal and held well above the leaves, 10' or more long, much branched and bearing millions of flowers
Gender: Bisexual flowers
Flower Color: White   **Fruit Size:** 1" diameter
Fruit Color: Olive green   **Irritant:** No

Comments: Gebang palm is one of about 8 *Corypha* species, two of which are cultivated in tropical landscapes for their spectacular flowering habits. After devoting 30 to 80 years to robust trunk and leaf development, all *Corypha* species produce a spectacular terminal inflorescence that erupts like a fountain high above the crown of leaves. As the fruits form over the course of a year, the leaves yellow and droop into brown obsolescence. By the time the palm's dramatic display of fecundity is over, the plant is dead. Even as young plants, gebang palms (and the related talipot) require a great deal of room for their massive canopies of large leaves (the largest among fan palms). The huge foliage of all *Corypha* species is valued in their native habitats for thatch, and palm sugar is made from sap collected from the trunk or inflorescence. Gebang palm often is slow to establish; growth quickens after trunk development. Though drought tolerant, it responds to irrigation during dry periods. Once known as *C. elata*.

Similar Species: *C. umbraculifera*, the talipot palm, is the largest of the coryphas. It has green leaf stems with small teeth, mostly at the margins of their bases. The inflorescence easily reaches 20' in height. Fruits are 1.25" in diameter. It is known in the "wild" (India and Sri Lanka) only in association with human settlement.

Scientific Name: *Cyrtostachys renda* (cer-tō-stak-ēz ren-dah)
Common Name(s): Red sealing wax palm, Lipstick palm

Typical Height: 15'
Subfamily: Arecoideae
Tribe: Areceae

Hardiness Zone: 11
Growth Rate: Slow
Origin: Malay Peninsula and Borneo

Landscape Characteristics

Salt Tolerance: Low
Drought Tolerance: Low to moderate
Soil Requirements: Widely adaptable
Light Requirements: Moderate, high
Nutritional Requirements: Moderate
Uses: Specimen plant, foliage plant
Propagation: Seed, germinating in 2-3 months with high heat; division
Human Hazards: None
Major Pest Problems: None
Major Disease or Physiological Problems: None

Morphology (Identifying Characteristics)

Habit: Clustering; each stem with 10 or fewer leaves
Trunk or Stem Characteristics: Slender, smooth, green or brownish; conspicuously ringed
Leaf Type: Pinnately compound, reduplicate; leaflets evenly spaced, narrow, and forming a V
Foliage Color: Green and red
Leaf Size: 3-4' long; leaflets 8-12" long, 1/2-2/3" wide
Petiole: Red, about 1' long
Crownshaft: Smooth, bright red (but variable), 2-3 feet long
Inflorescence: Red, short, slender, branched, borne below the crownshaft
Gender: Separate male and female flowers on the same inflorescence
Flower Color: Green
Fruit Size: 3/8" diameter
Fruit Color: Black
Irritant: No

Comments: Though few locations in the United States can provide a safe outdoor haven for the red sealing wax palm, its deserved reputation as one of the world's most beautiful palms justifies its treatment here. A denizen of moist, even swampy, rain forests, *C. renda* will not tolerate drought or drying winds, and pales at the slightest touch of winter chill. Nonetheless, the abiding beauty of its red crownshafts and leaf stems render it an item that few palm enthusiasts can resist. Except in the warm tropics, red sealing wax palm is best maintained as a container plant that can be easily protected when temperatures drop below 40° F. Seedlings generally take a long time to express the characteristic red coloration and are also variable in crownshaft color; faster results and guaranteed color can be obtained by carefully dividing established clumps.

Scientific Name: *Dictyosperma album* (dik-tē-ō-**sper**-mah **all**-bum)
Common Name(s): Hurricane palm, Princess palm

Typical Height: 30'
Subfamily: Arecoideae
Tribe: Areceae

Hardiness Zone: 10B-11
Growth Rate: Moderate
Origin: Mascarene Islands

Landscape Characteristics

Salt Tolerance: Moderate
Drought Tolerance: Moderate
Soil Requirements: Widely adaptable
Light Requirements: High
Nutritional Requirements: Moderate
Uses: Specimen tree
Propagation: Seed, germinating in 2-4 months
Human Hazards: None
Major Pest Problems: None
Major Disease or Physiological Problems:
Moderately susceptible to lethal yellowing
Cultivars: var. *aureum*: shorter trunk, orange-yellow
or reddish leaves on young plants; reddish-brown wax
on crownshaft

Morphology (Identifying Characteristics)

Habit: Solitary; canopy of 10-20 leaves
Trunk or Stem Characteristics: Relatively slender,
gray, ridged leaf scars and numerous vertical fissures,
swollen at base
Leaf Type: Pinnately compound, reduplicate; twisted
90° near tip; marginal reins frequent; leaflets numerous,
sharply pointed and ribbed
Foliage Color: Green, brown scales on underside of
leaflets
Leaf Size: 8-12' long; leaflets to 3' long, 2-3" wide
Petiole: .5-1' long; unarmed
Crownshaft: Wide; light green covered with gray to
brownish waxy scales
Inflorescence: 1.5' long; horn-like in bud
Gender: Male and female flowers on the same
inflorescence
Flower Color: Creamy yellow to reddish (depending
on variety)
Fruit Size: 1/2"
Fruit Color: Purple-black
Irritant: No

Comments: This beautiful palm, somewhat similar in appearance to
Archontophoenix (see comments on that species for distinguishing
characteristics), earns one of its common names by an alleged resistance to hurricane force winds. Drying winds can burn the foliage,
however, and a protective exposure is advisable in areas with low humidity. During periods of prolonged drought, supplementary irrigation is advantageous. Considered close to extinction in its native habitat, the princess palm is widely cultivated as an elegant vertical accent in tropical and subtropical landscapes. The variety *rubrum* has been combined by botanists with var. *aureum*.

Scientific Name: *Elaeis guineensis* (e-lay-iss ginn-e-en-sis)

Common Name(s): African oil palm

Typical Height: 35' (but capable of reaching over 50')
Subfamily: Arecoideae
Tribe: Cocoeae

Hardiness Zone: 10B-11
Growth Rate: Moderate
Origin: Africa

Landscape Characteristics

Salt Tolerance: Moderate
Drought Tolerance: Moderate
Soil Requirements: Widely adaptable
Light Requirements: High
Nutritional Requirements: Moderate
Uses: Specimen tree
Propagation: Seed, germinating in 2-5 months, tissue culture
Human Hazards: Spiny
Major Pest Problems: None
Major Disease or Physiological Problems: None
Cultivars: Various commercial varieties selected for oil characteristics

Morphology (Identifying Characteristics)

Habit: Solitary; canopy of 40-50 leaves
Trunk or Stem Characteristics: Heavy, often bulging at the middle; rings wide but do not circle the trunk; triangular leaf bases adhere for some time
Leaf Type: Pinnately compound, reduplicate, plumose; leaflets numerous, narrow and long, radiating in clusters; lower leaflets short and spine-like
Foliage Color: Green
Leaf Size: 12-16' long; leaflets 2-4' long, about 2" wide
Petiole: 2-5' long, broad, armed (peristent midribs of lower leaflets)
Crownshaft: None
Inflorescence: Short, dense, emerging from among the lower leaf axils; 4-12" long, with short, finger-like branches
Gender: Male and female flowers usually on different inflorescences
Flower Color: Cream
Fruit Size: 2" diameter
Fruit Color: Usually black and red, but some varieties have different colors
Irritant: No

Comments: The African oil palm is, after the coconut, the most important commercially exploited palm species. Commercial oils are extracted from both the fruit ("palm oil') and the seed ("palm kernal oil"). The oils are widely used for industrial as well as culinary purposes. Large plantations of this species are found throughout the tropics. While well adapted to warm humid climates world-wide, the robust size of the African oil palm limits its usefulness as a landscape palm. It is probably most appropriate for avenue and park plantings where its stately crown can be used to good advantage. Trees begin to bear fruit in about five years, which is held in very dense clusters of up to several hundred. The larges leaves (which appear every 2-3 weeks on established, well-growing trees) last for over 3 years. African oil palms adapt to poorly drained soils and will tolerate flooding for short periods.

Other Species: *E. oleifera*: this Central and South American oil palm is smaller than the African (to about 15'). The thick trunk creeps along the ground, rooting on its underside, for a number of years before turning upward.

Scientific Name: *Euterpe oleracea* (ū-ter-pē ō-ler-ā-see-ah)
Common Name(s): Assai palm

Typical Height: 60-80'
Subfamily: Arecoideae
Tribe: Areceae

Hardiness Zone: 11
Growth Rate: Fast
Origin: Brazil and north coast of South America

Landscape Characteristics

Salt Tolerance: Low
Drought Tolerance: Low
Soil Requirements: Acid
Light Requirements: Moderate, high (when mature)
Nutritional Requirements: Moderate
Uses: Specimen tree, edible fruit
Propagation: Seed, germinating in 1 month
Human Hazards: None
Major Pest Problems: None
Major Disease or Physiological Problems: None

Morphology (Identifying Characteristics)

Habit: Clustering; each stem with 8-15 leaves
Trunk or Stem Characteristics: Slender, green and brownish-gray, conspicuously ringed with wide, brownish leaf scars
Leaf Type: Pinnately compound, reduplicate, arching, with numerous narrow, drooping leaflets
Foliage Color: Green
Leaf Size: 6-10' long; leaflets 2-3' long, .5-1" wide
Petiole: 1' or less long; unarmed
Crownshaft: Long, slender, green
Inflorescence: 3' long, slender, much-branched, borne below the crownshaft
Gender: Separate male and female flowers on the same inflorescence
Flower Color: White
Fruit Size: 1" long
Fruit Color: Purple
Irritant: No

Comments: The assai palm is one of several dozen clustering or solitary rainforest species of *Euterpe* that occur throughout the warm American tropics. A thick, purple-colored drink (assai) is prepared from the ripe fruits that remains popular throughout Amazonian Brazil. Though fast-growing and very graceful in appearance, the assai palm is quite tender, and requires protection where freezing temperatures are periodically experienced. Like many wet rain forest palms, *E. oleracea* benefits from shade during its early years of growth, and a generous supply of moisture throughout its life. Regular fertilization is beneficial on poor, sandy soils, and alkalinity is not well tolerated. Protection from drying winds is also essential.

Other Species: *E. edulis*, the palmito, is a solitary-stemmed species from Brazil that is the commercial source of palm hearts (the innermost unexpanded leaves within the crownshaft), the harvest of which kills the palm.

Scientific Name: *Gaussia maya* (gowss-e-ah my-ah)
Common Name(s): Maya palm

Typical Height: 30'
Subfamily: Ceroxyloideae
Tribe: Hyophorbeae

Hardiness Zone: 10B-11
Growth Rate: Moderate
Origin: Guatemala, Belize and Mexico

°Landscape Characteristics

Salt Tolerance: Low
Drought Tolerance: Moderate
Soil Requirements: Widely adaptable
Light Requirements: Moderate, high
Nutritional Requirements: Moderate
Uses: Specimen tree
Propagation: Seed, germinating in 2 months
Human Hazards: Irritant
Major Pest Problems: None
Major Disease or Physiological Problems: None

Morphology (Identifying Characteristics)

Habit: Solitary; canopy of 5-7 leaves
Trunk or Stem Characteristics: Light brown (green just below crown) with widely-spaced and ridged leaf scars; root stubs at base
Leaf Type: Pinnately compound, reduplicate, ascending, with over 100 many-ranked leaflets that fall from the leaf stem as they age
Foliage Color: Green
Leaf Size: 9' long; leaflets 2' long, 2" wide
Petiole: 4' long, unarmed; base deeply notched on side opposite the blade
Crownshaft: Not well formed
Inflorescence: 3' long, with about a dozen short branches; borne low on the trunk; horn-like in bud
Gender: Separate male and female flowers on the same inflorescence
Flower Color: Greenish-white
Fruit Size: 3/4" diameter
Fruit Color: Red
Irritant: Yes

Comments: Formerly known as *Opsiandra maya*, the maya palm requires warmth and a steady supply of moisture for best growth, but is quite tolerant of a wide range of soil types. It makes an attractive specimen despite its relatively sparse crown of ascending leaves. It will tolerate full sun, but looks best if situated in part shade. The leaflets are arranged in many planes, giving the leaves a plume-like appearance which helps offset their small number. The first inflorescences of the maya palm remain in bud for several years as the trunk continues to grow, producing additional inflorescences above them. At some point, old and young buds begin to open sequentially from oldest to youngest, with the result that maya palms usually carry flowers and fruits at the same time and at all stages of development. Maya palm does have a reputation for blowing over in high winds. Three other species of *Gaussia* are known, from Puerto Rico, Mexico and Cuba.

Scientific Name: *Heterospathe elata* (het-er-ō-spay-thē ē-lah-tah)
Common Name(s): Sagisi palm

Typical Height: 40'
Subfamily: Arecoideae
Tribe: Cocoeae

Hardiness Zone: 10B-11
Growth Rate: Slow
Origin: Philippines

Landscape Characteristics

Salt Tolerance: Low
Drought Tolerance: Moderate
Soil Requirements: Widely adaptable
Light Requirements: Moderate, high
Nutritional Requirements: Moderate
Uses: Specimen tree, foliage plant
Propagation: Seed, germinating in 2 months
Human Hazards: None
Major Pest Problems: None
Major Disease or Physiological Problems: None

Morphology (Identifying Characteristics)

Habit: Solitary; canopy of 10-16 leaves
Trunk or Stem Characteristics: Smooth, with broad yellowish-brown ring scars, eventually gray and fissured, swollen at base
Leaf Type: Pinnately compound, reduplicate, with 130 tapered leaflets; stiffly arched and twisted sharply at the middle
Foliage Color: Green, but young leaves emerge pinkish-brown
Leaf Size: 5-10' long; leaflets 2-3' long, 1-1.5" wide
Petiole: 2' long, unarmed; base quite fibrous
Crownshaft: None
Inflorescence: 4' long, borne among the leaves, branched to several orders
Gender: Separate male and female flowers on the same inflorescence
Flower Color: White
Fruit Size: 1/4-1/2" diameter
Fruit Color: White
Irritant: No

Comments: The sagisi palm is one of several dozen rain forest palms in this genus, all natives of the southern Pacific region. It is finding wider use as a specimen tree in warm, relatively frost-free areas. It is valued for its attractive display of emergent leaf color, and shows promise as an interiorscape plant as well. Sagisi palm prospers with better than cursory maintenance; regular fertilization is essential on soils of low fertility. In the landscape it should not be situated where cold air is likely to settle during winter. The leaves are very sharply twisted such that the leaflets near the tip are held in a vertical plane.

Scientific Name: *Howea forsteriana* (how-ē-ah for-stir-ē-ann-ah)
Common Name(s): Kentia palm, Sentry palm

Typical Height: 30' (but can reach 60')
Subfamily: Arecoideae
Tribe: Cocoeae

Hardiness Zone: 9B-11
Growth Rate: Slow
Origin: Lord Howe Island, New South Wales, Australia

Salt Tolerance: Moderate
Drought Tolerance: Moderate
Soil Requirements: Widely adaptable
Light Requirements: Moderate, low, high only in temperate subtropical climates
Nutritional Requirements: Moderate
Uses: Specimen tree, foliage plant
Propagation: Seed, germinating in 2 months to 1 year, best with heat
Human Hazards: None
Major Pest Problems: Red scale
Major Disease or Physiological Problems: Phytophthora bud rot, stigmina and other fungal leaf spots

Morphology (Identifying Characteristics)

Habit: Solitary; canopy of about 3 dozen leaves
Trunk or Stem Characteristics: Swollen at base, gray, ring scars wavy and slightly raised
Leaf Type: Pinnately compound, reduplicate, arching; with numerous, evenly spaced, drooping leaflets
Foliage Color: Dark green above, lighter green below
Leaf Size: 12' long; leaflets about 2.5' long, 2" wide
Petiole: 4-5' long, unarmed, sheathing base becoming fibrous
Crownshaft: None
Inflorescence: 3.5' long, consisting of 3-7 spikes fused at the base
Gender: Male and female flowers on the same inflorescence
Flower Color: White
Fruit Size: 1.5" long
Fruit Color: Red
Irritant: No

Comments: Kentia palm is the world's most popular indoor palm, capable of retaining a good to excellent appearance for long durations under interiorscape conditions. However, as a landscape ornamental, the kentia is best reserved for cooler subtropical climates, as the species suffers with incessant heat and frequent drying winds. Light frosts are tolerated, but freezing temperatures will damage or even kill the palms. In cool, coastal climates such as in California, parts of Hawaii, and similar regions, kentias adapt well to full sun after attaining a reasonable size. If their culture is attempted in warmer or dryer areas, partial shade is recommended throughout their life. Despite its slow growth and the high cost of seed, kentia palm remains the reigning queen of interior palms due to its dark green, full and graceful crown of large leaves. As foliage plants they are frequently planted 2-3 per container, a practice which some feel disrupts the natural beauty of the palm.

Similar Species: *H. belmoreana* is a shorter, slightly less robust cousin of the kentia. Not as adaptable indoors as the kentia, the Belmore sentry palm has lighter green leaves and a 1-spiked inflorescence.

Scientific Name: *Hyophorbe lagenicaulis* (hī-ō-**fore**-bē lah-gen-ē-**caul**-is)
Common Name(s): Bottle palm

Typical Height: 12'
Subfamily: Ceroxyloideae
Tribe: Hyophorbeae

Hardiness Zone: 10B-11
Growth Rate: Slow
Origin: Round Island (Mascarenes)

Landscape Characteristics

Salt Tolerance: High
Drought Tolerance: Moderate
Soil Requirements: Widely adaptable
Light Requirements: Moderate, high
Nutritional Requirements: Moderate
Uses: Small specimen tree
Propagation: Seed, germinating in 3-6 months
Human Hazards: None
Major Pest Problems: None
Major Disease or Physiological Problems: Potassium deficiency (Florida)

Morphology (Identifying Characteristics)

Habit: Solitary; crown of 4-8 leaves
Trunk or Stem characteristics: Gray, smooth, closely ringed and usually vertically fissured, enormously swollen at base
Leaf Type: Pinnately compound, reduplicate, arching, with 140 leaflets held in an upward "V"; leaflets with several ribs
Foliage Color: Green to grayish green
Leaf Size: 9-12' long; leaflets about 2' long, 2" wide
Petiole: 8-10" long, unarmed, arching
Crownshaft: Smooth, green, waxy, broadest at base
Inflorescence: About 30" long, several borne in a circle just below crownshaft; densely branched; hornlike and erect in bud
Gender: Separate male and female flowers on the same inflorescence
Flower Color: Cream
Fruit Size: 1" long
Fruit Color: Black
Irritant: No

Comments: Bottle palm is cultivated throughout the world for its wonderfully novel shape and beautifully sculpted crownshaft. It is thus ironic that on Round Island in the Mascarene chain, the only known habitat for this popular palm, only 15 or so individuals remain. Despite the bizarrely swollen trunk, which most people assume to be a water storage adaptation, bottle palm requires irrigation during dry periods to look its best, especially if planted in full sun. Bottle palm thrives on heat and is very salt tolerant, but is severely damaged, if not killed outright, by freezing temperatures. Regular fertilization is essential to keep bottle palm's sparse canopy in good condition. In Florida it is particularly susceptible to potassium deficiency.

Scientific Name: *Hyophorbe verschaffeltii* (hī-ō-fore-bē ver-shah-fell-tē-ī)
Common Name(s): Spindle palm

Typical Height: 20'
Subfamily: Ceroxyloideae
Tribe: Hyophorbeae

Hardiness Zone: 10B-11
Growth Rate: Slow
Origin: Rodrigues Island (Mascarenes)

Salt Tolerance: High
Drought Tolerance: Moderate
Soil Requirements: Widely adaptable
Light Requirements: High
Nutritional Requirements: High
Uses: Small specimen tree
Propagation: Seed, germinating in 3-6 months
Human Hazards: None
Major Pest Problems: None
Major Disease or Physiological Problems: Potassium and magnesium deficiency (Florida), slight susceptibility to lethal yellowing

Morphology (Identifying Characteristics)

Habit: Solitary; crown of 5-10 leaves
Trunk or Stem Characteristics: Stout, gray, closely ringed, swollen at middle or just below crownshaft (but not excessively)
Leaf Type: Pinnately compound, reduplicate, arching; 100-150 leaflets held in several planes lack secondary ribs and droop slightly above the middle
Foliage Color: Bright green above, grayish green below
Leaf Size: 9-10' long; leaflets about 2.5' long, 2" wide
Petiole: To 1' long, unarmed
Crownshaft: Smooth, bright green, waxy, swollen at base
Inflorescence: 2.5' long, several borne in circle just below crownshaft, densely branched, hornlike and erect in bud
Gender: Separate male and female flowers on same inflorescence
Flower Color: Cream
Fruit Size: 3/4" long
Fruit Color: Orange to red
Irritant: No

Comments: Spindle palm grows slightly taller and is slightly hardier than the bottle palm. It can be easily separated from the latter by the less swollen trunk (which is never, on mature specimens, widest at the bottom), and the several-ranked leaflets that give the leaves a less formal appearance than those of bottle palm. Though still quite striking in appearance, spindle palm does not cast quite as novel an aspect as *H. lagenicaulis*, and thus combines more easily in the landscape with other palms. The leaves, especially on young plants, are noticeably triangular in arrangment on the stem. As with its sister species, spindle palm requires regular care to look its best, including supplementary irrigation during dry periods. It should be situated in full sun.

Scientific Name: *Hyphaene* spp. (hī-fē-nē)
Common Name(s): Gingerbread or Duom palms

Typical Height: 15-40'
Subfamily: Coryphoideae
Tribe: Borasseae

Hardiness Zone: 10B-11
Growth Rate: Slow
Origin: Africa, Arabia and India

Landscape Characteristics

Salt Tolerance: High
Drought Tolerance: High
Soil Requirements: Widely adaptable
Light Requirements: High
Nutritional Requirements: Low
Uses: Specimen tree
Propagation: Seed, germinating in 6 months or more; requires deep container
Human Hazards: Spiny
Major Pest Problems: None
Major Disease or Physiological Problems: None

Morphology (Identifying Characteristics)

Habit: Solitary or multi-trunked, rarely trunkless, branching; 20-30 leaves
Trunk or Stem characteristics: Black, deeply fissured, with brown leaf scars and tufts of fiber; covered with white to gray leaf bases when young
Leaf Type: Costapalmate, induplicate, round; arched and folded inward at tip of costa; divided 1/2 to 2/3 into several dozen pointed stiff segments
Foliage Color: Silvery-green, blue-green or glossy green
Leaf Size: Averaging 4' in diameter
Petiole: 3-4' long; edged with sharp, hooked black teeth that turn gray with age
Crownshaft: None
Inflorescence: Averaging 4' long; with short, thick branches
Gender: Separate male and female plants
Flower Color: Purplish-brown or yellow
Fruit Size: About 3" long
Fruit Color: Brown, black or yellow
Irritant: No

Comments: The gingerbread or duom palms comprise a group of about 10 species not yet well circumscribed from each other. They are a rarity within the palm family insofar as trunks of many of the species regularly branch well above the base. They are denizens of very arid regions by-and-large, but grow where sub-surface water can be mined by their deeply penetrating root systems. Their slow rate of growth and difficult handling has kept them from becoming well represented in nurseries and landscapes, but they are extremely tough palms, with some species that may even be hardy slightly north of USDA Zone 10. Thriving cultivated specimens of several species can be found in south Florida, southern California, and other sub-tropical and tropical regions. The sizable fruits are edible, though barely palatable, and have been utilized as subsistence or survival food. They are often pear- or top-shaped. A few of the occasionally encountered species and their place of origin are: *H. compressa* (East Africa), *H. thebaica* (North Africa) and *H. coriacea* (Southeast Africa).

Scientific Name: *Jubaea chilensis* (jū-bē-ah chill-en-sis)
Common Name(s): Chilean wine palm

Typical Height: 50-80'
Subfamily: Arecoideae
Tribe: Cocoeae

Hardiness Zone: 9-10A (California and other Mediterranean-type climatic zones only)
Growth Rate: Slow
Origin: Chile

Landscape Characteristics

Salt Tolerance: Low
Drought Tolerance: High (once established)
Soil Requirements: Widely adaptable
Light Requirements: High
Nutritional Requirements: Moderate
Uses: Specimen tree; sap collected for sugar and alcohol (palm is killed)
Propagation: Seed, germinating erratically in 6 months to over a year
Human Hazards: None
Major Pest Problems: None
Major Disease or Physiological Problems: None

Morphology (Identifying Characteristics)

Habit: Solitary, robust; massive crown of several dozen leaves
Trunk or Stem Characteristics: Thick (4-6' diameter), dark gray, conspicuously marked with raised, diamond shaped leaf scars
Leaf Type: Pinnately compound, reduplicate, stiff, spreading; with several hundred narrow, pointed leaflets that split at their tips
Foliage Color: Dull green above, gray below
Leaf Size: 6-12' long; leaflets 2' long, 1" wide
Petiole: Short, with hairy fibers at margins
Crownshaft: None
Inflorescence: About 4' long, densely branched, borne among the lower leaves
Gender: Separate male and female flowers on the same inflorescence
Flower Color: Purple
Fruit Size: 1.25" diameter
Fruit Color: Orange-yellow
Irritant: No

Comments: This rare and amazing species quite possibly has the thickest trunk of any palm so far known. Chilean wine palm occurs in a few coastal valleys in Chile that remain devoid of extremes of both heat and cold. Native populations were exploited for the sugary sap for many years. This practice severely reduced their numbers since the trunk is cut down at harvest. The species is now protected by law. Sap reportedly can be collected from felled trunks for up to two years. Chilean wine palm grows poorly in hot, humid tropical and subtropical climates. It is best suited for coastal California, the Mediterranean coast, and similar climatic zones in Australia and South Africa.

Scientific Name: *Latania loddigesii* (la-tane-ē-ah lō-deh-gēz-ē-ī)
Common Name(s): Blue latan palm

Typical Height: 30'
Subfamily: Coryphoideae
Tribe: Borasseae

Hardiness Zone: 10B-11
Growth Rate: Slow
Origin: Mauritius Island (Mascarenes)

Landscape Characteristics

Salt Tolerance: Moderate
Drought Tolerance: High
Soil Requirements: Widely adaptable
Light Requirements: High
Nutritional Requirements: Moderate
Uses: Specimen tree
Propagation: Seed (which must be fresh), germinating in 1-2 months
Human Hazards: None
Major Pest Problems: Palmetto weevils
Major Disease or Physiological Problems: Slight susceptibility to lethal yellowing

Morphology (Identifying Characteristics)

Habit: Solitary; canopy of 1-2 dozen leaves
Trunk or Stem Characteristics: Grayish-brown, swollen at base, slightly bulged near wavy narrow ring scars
Leaf Type: Costapalmate, stiffly folded, divided to 1/2 into about 30 stiff, unsplit segments with finely-toothed margins becoming smooth with age; hastula pointed and flat
Foliage Color: Blue-green, waxy, almost woolly below; red veins when young
Leaf Size: 6-8' wide, segments several feet long, 3" wide
Petiole: 4-6' long, bluish (red when young), variably toothed (when young); base split; scurfy
Crownshaft: None
Inflorescence: 3-6' long, from among the leaves; males with clusters of short, clubby branches, females with single short branches
Gender: Separate male and female plants
Flower Color: Brownish-yellow
Fruit Size: 2-3" long, 1" wide
Fruit Color: Brownish-green
Irritant: No

Comments: The latan palms are lovely tropical fan palms, as striking when young, due to their specific coloration, as they are as mature specimens. Much of the color fades as these palms age, thus older individuals of the different species can be difficult to distinguish from each other without attention to some rather inconspicuous features. Blue latans are highlighted with mottled blue, most of the color concentrated in the leaf stems and veins. It is also the "scurfiest" of the species, with a dense deposit of woolly wax on the leaf undersides. Small seedlings can be an intense purple-red, and easily confused with red latan. As they age, they become less red than the red latan. The seed of the blue latan has a distinctive, convoluted surface ornamentation at its broader end, and sure identity is best confirmed by observation of seeds. All latan palms are adapted to a seasonally dry tropical climate, and prosper with hot, wet summers and warm but drier winters. In the wild, they often occur close to the shore (but on cliffs and in canyons where they would not receive direct salt spray). Older specimens are at some risk in areas known to harbor lethal yellowing disease.

Scientific Name: *Latania lontaroides* (la-**tane**-ē-ah   lon-tah-**roy**-dēz)

Common Name(s): Red latan palm

Typical Height: 30'
Subfamily: Coryphoideae
Tribe: Borasseae

Hardiness Zone: 10B-11
Growth Rate: Slow
Origin: Reunion Island (Mascarenes)

Juvenile (foreground), mature (background).

Landscape Characteristics

Salt Tolerance: Moderate
Drought Tolerance: High
Soil Requirements: Widely adaptable
Light Requirements: High
Nutritional Requirements: Moderate
Uses: Specimen tree
Propagation: Seed (which must be fresh), germinating in 1-2 months
Human Hazards: None
Major Pest Problems: Palmetto weevils
Major Disease or Physiological Problems: Slight to moderate susceptibility to lethal yellowing

Morphology (Identifying Characteristics)

Habit: Solitary; canopy of 12-24 leaves
Trunk or Stem Characteristics: Grayish-brown, swollen at base, bulged near the wide ring scars
Leaf Type: Costapalmate, stiffly folded, divided to 1/2 into about 30 unsplit segments with finely-toothed margins (fades with age); hastula broad, blunt and raised
Foliage Color: Gray-green and slightly waxy (red and shiny green when young); red margins and veins
Leaf Size: 6-8' wide, segments several feet long, 3" wide
Petiole: 4-6' long, reddish, slightly toothed (when young); base sheath split; scurfy
Crownshaft: None
Inflorescence: 3-6' long, from among the leaves; males with clusters of short, clubby branches; females with single short branches
Gender: Separate male and female plants
Flower Color: Brownish-yellow
Fruit Size: 2-3" long, 1" wide
Fruit Color: Brownish-green
Irritant: No

Comments: The red latan eventually loses most the red foliar highlights that make it such a distinctive young specimen. It can be distinguished from the blue latan by its pointed and upraised hastula on the upper leaf surface, less waxy scurf on the leaf underside, and wide leaf scars on a gray trunk. The seed lacks the attractive sculpturing found on that of the blue latan palm. Culture is the same as for the blue latan.

Other Species: The yellow latan (*L. verschaffeltii*), from Rodriguez Island, has yellow to yellow-orange petioles and leaf veins. The hastula is small, blunt and flat. The trunk only rarely bulges around the leaf scars. The dark seeds are three lobed and have a conspicuous ridge running down the middle. Hybrids are known between it and the red latan.

Scientific Name: *Licuala grandis* (lik-oo-ah-lah grand-is)
Common Name(s): Licuala palm

Typical Height: 8'
Subfamily: Coryphoideae
Tribe: Corypheae

Hardiness Zone: 10B-11
Growth Rate: Slow
Origin: New Hebrides Islands

Landscape Characteristics

Salt Tolerance: Low
Drought Tolerance: Low
Soil Requirements: Widely adaptable
Light Requirements: Medium
Nutritional Requirements: High
Uses: Small tree
Propagation: Seed, germinating in 3-6 months with heat
Human Hazards: Spiny
Major Pest Problems: None
Major Disease or Physiological Problems: None

Morphology (Identifying Characteristics)

Habit: Solitary; canopy of 10-20 leaves
Trunk or Stem Characteristics: Slender, gray-brown, ridged, with non-circling leaf scars; covered with fiber and projecting leaf bases for many years
Leaf Type: Palmate, induplicate, almost circular, usually undivided, densely pleated along ribs
Foliage Color: Green, shiny
Leaf Size: About 3' wide
Petiole: About 3' long, armed with hooked teeth in the lower 2/3
Crownshaft: None
Inflorescence: 6' long, loosely branched, produced from among the leaves
Gender: Bisexual flowers
Flower Color: White
Fruit Size: l/2" diameter
Fruit Color: Red
Irritant: No

Comments: *Licuala grandis*, with its seemingly perfectly circular leaves (in fact, they are not) is one of the most attractive palms available for tropical landscapes. The corrugated and (usually) unsegmented leaves are a bright shiny green and immediately catch the eye with their elegant and symmetrical shape. *Licuala grandis* is a wet rainforest understory plant, and requires part shade for best appearance, in a situation protected from drying winds. It should receive irrigation during prolonged dry periods. A well-drained but organic soil is ideal; on sandy soils, maintenance of an organic mulch is strongly recommended. This slow-growing species can also be maintained for many years in a large container or tub on a shaded patio.

Similar Species: The genus *Licuala* consists of 100 or more single-stemmed or clustering species that are not well understood taxonomically. The following solitary species are occasionally cultivated: *L. ramsayi* (Australia, New Guinea) can reach 20' and bears circular leaves that eventually divide into several irregular segments. *L. lauterbachii* (New Guinea) is a tender species that grows to 12' and bears nearly circular leaves split into about 30 segments. *L. paludosa* (Malaysia and SE Asia) resembles a single-stemmed spiny licuala (*L. spinosa*).

<h2 style="text-align:center">Scientific Name: Licuala spinosa (lik-oo-ah-lah spy-nos-ah)</h2>
<h2 style="text-align:center">Common Name(s): Spiny licuala</h2>

Typical Height: 12'
Subfamily: Coryphoideae
Tribe: Corypheae

Hardiness Zone: 10B-11
Growth Rate: Slow
Origin: Malaysia, Philippines, Indonesia

Landscape Characteristics

Salt Tolerance: Low
Drought Tolerance: Moderate
Soil Requirements: Widely adaptable
Light Requirements: Moderate
Nutritional Requirements: Moderate
Uses: Shrub
Propagation: Seed, germinating in 3-6 months with heat
Human Hazards: Spiny
Major Pest Problems: None
Major Disease or Physiological Problems: None

Morphology (Identifying Characteristics)

Habit: Clumping; each stem with about 10 leaves
Trunk or Stem characteristics: Slender, covered with fiber and leaf bases
Leaf Type: Palmate, circular, divided deeply into 20 or so wedge-shaped segments that are toothed at their truncated tips
Foliage Color: Green, shiny
Leaf Size: About 3' wide; segments several inches wide
Petiole: 3-5' long, armed with sharp, hooked teeth
Crownshaft: None
Inflorescence: 4-8' long, loosely branched
Gender: Bisexual flowers
Flower color: White
Fruit Size: 1/2" diameter
Fruit Color: Red
Irritant: No

Comments: Despite the ferocious armament along the leaf stems and its slow rate of growth, spiny licuala is prized for its attractively segmented circular leaves. It is one of more sun-tolerant species in the genus, but leaves maintain their best appearance with some shade. Its water demands are directly proportional to the amount of sunlight the palm receives. Spiny licuala also appears to be slightly hardier than *L. grandis*.

Similar Species: *L. rumphii* (Eastern Indonesia) is a tightly clumping species slightly smaller than spiny licuala. The leaves form about 3/4 of a circle and are divided to the stem into several broad segments. *L. gracilis* (Java) is a dwarf clumper that rarely exceeds 5' in height.

Scientific Name: *Livistona australis* (liv-iss-tōne-ah os-tral-iss)

Common Name(s): Australian fan palm

Typical Height: 40'
Subfamily: Coryphoideae
Tribe: Corypheae

Hardiness Zone: 9-11
Growth Rate: Slow
Origin: Australia

Landscape Characteristics

Salt Tolerance: Moderate
Drought Tolerance: High
Soil Requirements: Widely adaptable
Light Requirements: Moderate, high
Nutritional Requirements: Moderate
Uses: Specimen tree
Propagation: Seed, germinating in 1-2 months
Human Hazards: Spiny (chiefly when young)
Major Pest Problems: None
Major Disease or Physiological Problems: Potassium deficiency (Florida)

Morphology (Identifying Characteristics)

Habit: Solitary, robust; canopy of 30-50 leaves
Trunk or Stem Characteristics: Gray or brown, closely ringed with ridged leaf scars, fissured; leaf bases and fiber persist for several years
Leaf Type: Costapalmate, induplicate, thin-textured, circular; divided to about 2/3 into numerous, deeply split segments that droop at their tips
Foliage Color: Deep, glossy green; sometimes tinged brown
Leaf Size: 6-8' diameter; segments 3' long, 1.5" wide
Petiole: About 6' long, narrow, marginally toothed on young specimens
Crownshaft: None
Inflorescence: About 4' long, shortly branched, borne among the leaves
Gender: Bisexual flowers (sometimes function as males only)
Flower Color: Creamy yellow
Fruit Size: 3/4" long
Fruit Color: Reddish-brown to black
Irritant: No

Comments: After Chinese fan palm, Australian fan palm is probably the hardiest *Livistona* species in wide cultivation. It grows considerably taller than Chinese fan palm, however, and can be distinguished from that species by its conspicuously ridged trunk. It also does not appear to be susceptible to lethal yellowing. Early Australian settlers harvested the heart for cabbage, fashioned hats and baskets from the leaves, and utilized the trunks for light construction. Aborigines made fishing lines and nets from leaf fiber, used the leaves for roofing, and pieces of the outer trunk to make spear heads. Australian fan palm is one of the most carefree species in the genus and adapts well to a wide variety of soil types.

Scientific Name: *Livistona chinensis* (liv-iss-tōne-ah chey-nen-sis)

Common Name(s): Chinese fan palm

Typical Height: 25'
Subfamily: Coryphoideae
Tribe: Corypheae

Hardiness Zone: 9-11
Growth Rate: Slow
Origin: China, southern Japan

Landscape Characteristics

Salt Tolerance: Moderate
Drought Tolerance: High
Soil Requirements: Widely adaptable
Light Requirements: Moderate, high
Nutritional Requirements: Moderate
Uses: Specimen tree
Propagation: Seed, germinating in 1-2 months
Human Hazards: Spiny (variable)
Major Pest Problems: None
Major Disease or Physiological Problems: Moderate susceptibility to lethal yellowing, ganoderma
Cultivars: Var. *subglobosa* has been applied to wild forms with spherical (rather than ovoid) fruits

Morphology (Identifying Characteristics)

Habit: Solitary; canopy of 30-50 leaves
Trunk or Stem Characteristics: Brown initially, gray with age, closely ringed with incomplete leaf scars, eventually corky below
Leaf Type: Costapalmate, divided to about 2/3 into 60-100 deeply split segments that are pendant in their lower half
Foliage Color: Olive green
Leaf Size: About 6' diameter; segments 3-4' long, 2 inches wide
Petiole: 6' long, teeth (if present) along margins of lower half
Crownshaft: None
Inflorescence: 6' feet long, produced from among the leaves, densely branched
Gender: Bisexual flowers
Flower Color: Cream
Fruit Size: .5-1" long
Fruit Color: Grayish-blue
Irritant: No

Comments: By far the most widely planted member of the genus, Chinese fan palm makes a slow-growing but handsome specimen, forming a wide-spreading attractive crown even as a young plant. This has even led to their use as a ground cover in landscaping, an outrageous practice since at least half of the palms will require removal as they age. The long leaf segment tips hang gracefully giving the canopy a weeping appearance. They are tolerant of relatively infertile soils, but respond favorably to good nutrition. It is probably the hardiest of the livistonas, and can withstand several degrees below freezing without any damage. Full sun is best for the Chinese fan palm; in anything more than light shade, the leaves have a tendency to "stretch."

Scientific Name: *Livistona decipiens* (liv-iss-tōne-ah dē-sip-ē-enz)
Common Name(s): Ribbon fan palm

Typical Height: 30'
Subfamily: Coryphoideae
Tribe: Corypheae

Hardiness Zone: 9-11
Growth Rate: Slow to moderate
Origin: Australia

Landscape Characteristics

Salt Tolerance: Moderate
Drought Tolerance: High
Soil Requirements: Widely adaptable
Light Requirements: Moderate, high
Nutritional Requirements: Moderate
Uses: Specimen tree
Propagation: Seed, germinating in 1-2 months
Human Hazards: Spiny
Major Pest Problems: None
Major Disease or Physiological Problems: None

Morphology (Identifying Characteristics)

Habit: Solitary, robust; canopy of 40-60 leaves
Trunk or Stem Characteristics: Brown, with circling reddish-brown ring scars, slightly swollen at base
Leaf Type: Costapalmate, with long costa, induplicate; divided deeply into many folded segments that split at their middle and hang down gracefully
Foliage Color: Deep green above, waxy gray below
Leaf Size: 7-9' wide; segments 4-5' long, 3/4" wide
Petiole: 6' long; armed with small, sharp teeth
Crownshaft: None
Inflorescence: 4' long, from among the leaves
Gender: Bisexual flowers
Flower Color: Yellow
Fruit Size: 5/8" diameter
Fruit Color: Dull black
Irritant: No

Comments: Ribbon fan palm most closely resembles Australian fan palm but does not grow as tall as the latter and bears larger leaves. It is most notable for its deeply divided leaves, the long segments of which hang downward like a curtain for several feet. This effect is best exhibited in a sheltered position; in the open the leaves tend to become tattered by the wind.

Scientific Name: *Livistona mariae* (liv-iss-tōne-ah mahr-ĭ-ē)
Common Name(s): Central Australian fan palm

Typical Height: 40'
Subfamily: Coryphoideae
Tribe: Corypheae

Hardiness Zone: 10A-10B
Growth Rate: Moderate
Origin: Australia

Landscape Characteristics

Salt Tolerance: Moderate
Drought Tolerance: High
Soil Requirements: Widely adaptable
Light Requirements: High
Nutritional Requirements: Moderate
Uses: Specimen tree
Propagation: Seed, usually germinating within 3 months
Human Hazards: Spiny
Major Pest Problems: None
Major Disease or Physiological Problems: Potassium deficiency

Morphology (Identifying Characteristics)

Habit: Solitary; canopy of several dozen leaves
Trunk or Stem Characteristics: Covered with burlap-like fiber and protruding leaf bases for some years, eventually gray and ringed; swollen at base
Leaf Type: Costapalmate, induplicate; divided to more than half the diameter; tips drooping
Foliage Color: Dark green; purple-red when young (especially in full sun)
Leaf Size: 6' or more in diameter
Petiole: Long, to 6'; sharply toothed in the lower half
Crownshaft: None
Inflorescence: Long, erect, branched
Gender: Bisexual flowers
Flower Color: Yellow
Fruit Size: 1"
Fruit Color: Black
Irritant: No

Comments: *Livistona mariae* is known only from the Alice Springs area in central Australia. This is hot, dry territory, but the palm occurs in close proximity to year-round water from springs and appears very adaptable to moist, subtropical conditions. It is among the largest-leafed *Livistona* species and requires ample room for its sizable canopy. The leaves of young plants turn purplish-red in full sun and also are toothed on their margins.

Scientific Name: *Livistona rotundifolia* (liv-iss-tōne-ah rō-tun-deh-fō-lē-ah)
Common Name(s): Footstool palm, Round leaf fan palm

Typical Height: 35'
Subfamily: Coryphoideae
Tribe: Corypheae

Hardiness Zone: 10B-11
Growth Rate: Moderate
Origin: Philippines, Indonesia

Salt Tolerance: Low
Drought Tolerance: Moderate
Soil Requirements: Widely adaptable
Light Requirements: Moderate, high
Nutritional Requirements: Moderate
Uses: Specimen tree, foliage plant
Propagation: Seed, germinating in 1-2 months
Human Hazards: Spiny
Major Pest Problems: None
Major Disease or Physiological Problems:
Slight to moderate susceptibility to lethal yellowing, ganoderma

Morphology (Identifying Characteristics)

Habit: Solitary; canopy of 30-50 leaves
Trunk or Stem Characteristics: Smooth, pale gray with reddish leaf scars, fissured; covered with fiber and wedge-shaped leaf bases for many years
Leaf Type: Costapalmate, induplicate; divided to 1/2 or less into into 60 or more straight, shortly split segments
Foliage Color: Deep glossy green
Leaf Size: 5-7' wide; segments about 2" wide
Petiole: 6-8' long, slender; armed with curved teeth, especially in lower half.
Crownshaft: None
Inflorescence: 8' long, split into 3 main branches each with many short secondary branches
Gender: Bisexual flowers
Flower Color: Yellow
Fruit Size: 3/4" long
Fruit Color: Brownish-black (red before ripening)
Irritant: No

Comments: This beautiful but less hardy *Livistona* makes a lovely container specimen when young, the leaves forming almost perfect circles. Juvenile leaves are also only shallowly divided. Unlike many of the hardier species, the segments of the bright green, glossy leaves do not droop regularly. The trunk, whether covered with a mat of fiber and protruding leaf bases or clean and revealing the red ring scars, is also striking in appearance.

Similar Species: *L. robinsoniana* (Philippines) is similar in aspect but taller growing.

Scientific Name: *Livistona saribus* (liv-iss-tōne-ah sar-ē-buss)
Common Name(s): Taraw palm

Typical Height: 60'
Subfamily: Coryphoideae
Tribe: Corypheae

Hardiness Zone: 10A-11
Growth Rate: Moderate
Origin: Southeast Asia, Indonesia & Philippines

Landscape Characteristics

Salt Tolerance: Moderate
Drought Tolerance: High
Soil Requirements: Widely adaptable
Light Requirements: Moderate, high
Nutritional Requirements: Moderate
Uses: Specimen tree
Propagation: Seed, germinating within two months
Human Hazards: Spiny
Major Pest Problems: None
Major Disease or Physiological Problems: None

Morphology (Identifying Characteristics)

Habit: Solitary; canopy of several dozen leaves
Trunk or Stem Characteristics: Robust, pale gray, ringed; wedge-shaped leaf bases adhere when young
Leaf Type: Costapalmate, induplicate; divided about mid-depth into forked segments that droop at the tips
Foliage Color: Deep green
Leaf Size: 4-5' in diameter
Petiole: To 6' long; armed with long, straight, sharp teeth, especially in lower half
Crownshaft: None
Inflorescence: 5' or more long, openly branched
Gender: Bisexual flowers
Flower Color: Yellow
Fruit Size: 3/4"
Fruit Color: Glossy blue-gray, often with white spots
Irritant: No

Comments: This southeast Asian fan palm appears well adapted to Florida conditions. It responds well to irrigation and fertilization when young. The dense crown requires ample room for development.

Scientific Name: *Nannorrhops ritchiana* (nan-or-rops rit-chē-ann-ah)

Common Name(s): Mazari palm

Typical Height: 10' (range of 5-25')
Subfamily: Coryphoideae
Tribe: Corypheae

Hardiness Zone: 8-11
Growth Rate: Slow
Origin: Afghanistan, Pakistan to Arabia

Landscape Characteristics

Salt Tolerance: Moderate
Drought Tolerance: High
Soil Requirements: Widely adaptable if well-drained
Light Requirements: High
Nutritional Requirements: Low
Uses: Shrub
Propagation: Seed, germinating slowly
Human Hazards: None
Major Pest Problems: None
Major Disease or Physiological Problems: Slight susceptibility to lethal yellowing, ganoderma

Morphology (Identifying Characteristics)

Habit: Clustering, branching; stems die back after flowering; 30-40 leaves
Trunk or Stem Characteristics: Short, mostly underground, prostrate (erect with age); thick, covered with leaf stem bases and orange fiber
Leaf Type: Costapalmate, stiff, twisted; divided deeply into about 30 segments that split for half their length
Foliage Color: Blue-green
Leaf Size: 4' wide; segments 4' long, 1.5' wide
Petiole: 1-3' long, unarmed or with small marginal teeth
Crownshaft: None
Inflorescence: 4-6" long, from the apex of the stem and held high above leaves, much-branched
Gender: Bisexual flowers
Flower Color: White
Fruit Size: 1/2" diameter
Fruit Color: Brownish orange
Irritant: No; edible

Comments: This unusual species may be the hardiest of all palms, adapted through its native range to extremes of summer heat and winter cold. The mazari palm is also extremely slow-growing, even in very mild winter areas. As each stem prepares to flower, new leaves emerge progressively smaller. The branched flowerstem is produced from the tip of the stem and towers above the leaf canopy. After fruiting, the stem eventually dies back, but not before branching just below the crown. With its habit of both clustering below ground and branching above, the mazari palm can form a specimen of impressive spread if not height. The powdery blue-green leaves create an eye-catching accent. Throughout its desert range, it is a source of palm cabbage, and fiber for weaving and rope manufacture. The fruits are also eaten.

Scientific Name: *Neodypsis decaryi* (nē-ō-dip-sis dē-car-yī)
Common Name(s): Triangle palm

Typical Height: 25'
Subfamily: Arecoideae
Tribe: Areceae

Hardiness Zone: 10B-11
Growth Rate: Moderate
Origin: Madagascar

Landscape Characteristics

Salt Tolerance: Low
Drought Tolerance: High (when established)
Soil Requirements: Widely adaptable
Light Requirements: Moderate, high
Nutritional Requirements: Moderate
Uses: Specimen tree
Propagation: Seed, germinating in 1-2 months
Human Hazards: None
Major Pest Problems: None
Major Disease or Physiological Problems: Potassium deficiency (Florida); bacterial bud rot if overwatered, slight susceptibility to lethal yellowing

Morphology (Identifying Characteristics)

Habit: Solitary, robust; canopy of about 20 leaves
Trunk or Stem Characteristics: Short, dark brown, with narrow, gray leaf scars; leaves radiate out in three planes
Leaf Type: Pinnately compound, reduplicate, stiff, curved downward near tip; 100-200 pointed leaflets forming a narrow "V"; marginal reins frequent
Foliage Color: Blue-green; patches of red scales on underside of leaflets
Leaf Size: 8-10' long; leaflets 1-2" long, 1.5" wide
Petiole: About 1' long, unarmed; bases covered with dark brownish-red scurf
Crownshaft: Not really formed; overlapping and bulging leaf bases form distinctive triangular configuration
Inflorescence: 4-5' long, emerging from among the lower leaves, branched
Gender: Separate male and female flowers on the same infloresence
Flower Color: Yellow
Fruit Size: 1" long
Fruit Color: Yellow-green
Irritant: No

Comments: The triangle palm is one of the most unique of all landscape palms in appearance, due to the very precise three-planed arrangement of the leaves. Though a true crownshaft is not formed, the tightly overlapping and bulging leaf bases form a stocky triangle above the short trunk. The leaf bases are covered with brownish red hairs that easily rub off. Long "reins" frequently hang down from the blue-green leaves. The stiff, planar canopy of triangle palm results in a very bold and formal appearance that dominates the area of the landscape it inhabits. Consequently, its placement should be carefully considered. Though drought tolerant in humid subtropical and tropical zones once established, triangle palm requires periodic irrigation as it settles into place. In dry summer regions such as California, irrigation is essential. The planting site should be well-drained, and regular fertilization is a must on poor, infertile soils. The leaves are damaged at temperatures below freezing, and older specimens may require 2 years or more to renew a full canopy after a severe freeze.

Scientific Name: *Neodypsis lastelliana* (nē-ō-dip-sis lah-stell-ē-ann-ah)
Common Name(s): Teddy bear palm, Redneck palm

Typical Height: 30'
Subfamily: Arecoideae
Tribe: Areceae

Hardiness Zone: 10B-11
Growth Rate: Moderate
Origin: Madagascar

Landscape Characteristics

Salt Tolerance: Low
Drought Tolerance: High (once established)
Soil Requirements: Widely adaptable
Light Requirements: High
Nutritional Requirements: Moderate
Uses: Specimen tree
Propagation: Seed, germinating in several months
Human Hazards: None
Major Pest Problems: None
Major Disease or Physiological Problems: None
Cultivars: Var. *darianii* (pictured): named for the California collector Mardy Darian, has very well developed crownshaft "fur"

Morphology (Identifying Characteristics)

Habit: Solitary
Trunk or Stem Characteristics: Brown, attractively ringed with wide, whitish ring scars
Leaf Type: Pinnately compound, reduplicate, erect
Foliage Color: Bright green
Leaf Size: 6' long; leaflets 1-1.5' long, 1.5" wide
Petiole: Short, .5-1" long, green
Crownshaft: Loosely formed; leaf stems bases covered with fur-like rust-red scales
Inflorescence: Short, borne from lower leaf axils
Gender: Separate male and female flowers on the same inflorescence
Flower Color: White
Fruit Size: About 1"
Fruit Color: Yellowish-orange
Irritant: No

Comments: This relative of the triangle palm has been grown very successfully in southern California and is now becoming available in south Florida. The crownshaft of leaf bases is attractively covered with rust-red hairs. As the palms age, if older bases are pulled away, a waxy underlay of white to bluish-white marks the younger ring scars. The canopy of redneck palm is bright green and spreading; the leaflets stand at right angles from the rachis.

Scientific Name: *Phoenix canariensis* (fē-niks can-ā-rē-en-sis)
Common Name(s): Canary Island date

Typical Height: 40'
Subfamily: Coryphoideae
Tribe: Phoeniceae

Hardiness Zone: 9-11
Growth Rate: Slow
Origin: Canary Islands

Landscape Characteristics

Salt Tolerance: Moderate
Drought Tolerance: High
Soil Requirements: Widely adaptable, well-drained
Light Requirements: High
Nutritional Requirements: Moderate
Uses: Specimen tree
Propagation: Seed, germinating in 2-3 months
Human Hazards: Spiny
Major Pest Problems: Palmetto weevils, palm-leaf skeletonizer
Major Disease or Physiological Problems: Lethal yellowing, magnesium deficiency, ganoderma, stigmina leaf spot, graphiola false smut, phytophthora bud rot

Morphology (Identifying Characteristics)

Habit: Solitary, massive; canopy of 50-100 leaves
Trunk or Stem Characteristics: Thick, to 3' in diameter, with distinctive diamond leaf scar pattern; swollen mass of aerial roots often forms at base
Leaf Type: Pinnately compound, induplicate; stiffly arched, sometimes twisted; several hundred narrow leaflets
Foliage Color: Dull deep green
Leaf Size: 10-20; leaflets about 1.5' long, 1" wide
Petiole: Short, strongly armed with leaflet spines in lower third
Crownshaft: None
Inflorescence: 3-4' long, orange, densely branched
Gender: Separate male and female plants
Flower Color: Yellow
Fruit Size: 3/4"
Fruit Color: Orange
Irritant: No (edible but not very palatable)

Comments: Canary Island date palm is highly prized for its formal aspect in the landscape which complements Mediterranean style architecture, and for its hardiness which allows its use thoroughout most of Florida and parts of California and Arizona. The leaf scar pattern on the trunk is very ornamental. The spread of Canary Island dates require ample room for development even when the palms are young. Extremely tough and durable, this species endures dry conditions and, with the exception of easily correctable magnesium deficiency, poor soils as well. Poorly drained sites, however, should be avoided. Over-irrigation may increase susceptibility to various fungal diseases. Transplanting large specimens should be handled carefully; stressed plants are easily invaded by palmetto weevils which quickly destroy the irreplacable "heart." A fair number of the Canary Island date palms sold are actually hybrids of this and other *Phoenix* species. Blue-green leafed specimens sold as Canary Islands are usually hybrid individuals.

Scientific Name: *Phoenix dactylifera* (fē-niks dak-till-if-er-ah)
Common Name(s): Date palm

Typical Height: 70'
Subfamily: Coryphoideae
Tribe: Phoeniceae

Hardiness Zone: 9-11
Growth Rate: Slow
Origin: North Africa, but exact origin unknown

Landscape Characteristics

Salt Tolerance: High
Drought Tolerance: High
Soil Requirements: Widely adaptable
Light Requirements: High
Nutritional Requirements: Moderate
Uses: Specimen tree
Propagation: Seed, germinating in 2-3 months; suckers, tissue culture
Human Hazards: Spiny
Major Pest Problems: Scales
Major Disease or Physiological Problems: Moderately susceptible to lethal yellowing, stigmina leaf spot, graphiola false smut
Cultivars: Hundreds if not thousands of cultivars throughout the Middle East selected largely for fruit characteristics. Common cultivars used in landscaping include 'Medjool', Zahedi', and 'Deglet Noor'

Morphology (Identifying Characteristics)

Habit: Slowly clustering (main trunk dominates for many years), 20-40 leaves
Trunk or Stem Characteristics: Robust, gray and patterned with broad leaf scars after persistant leaf bases fall; offsets (suckers) often at base
Leaf Type: Pinnately compound, induplicate, erect at first, then drooping; with 200+ stiff, pointed leaflets, the lower ones modified into spines
Foliage Color: Gray-green
Leaf Size: To 20' long; leaflets 1-2' long, 1" wide
Petiole: 4' feet long, armed with leaflet spines
Crownshaft: None
Inflorescence: 4' long, densely branched, borne from among the leaves
Gender: Separate male and female plants
Flower color: White
Fruit Size: 1.2-1.5" long
Fruit Color: Yellow, orange or red
Irritant: No; edible

Comments: The edible or "true" date palm is becoming much more widely used in landscaping than previously, especially since large specimens have become available from date groves in California and Arizona that have ceased production. They are adaptable landscape palms, with a broad range of environmental tolerance, but fruit poorly in the humid tropics and subtropics. The canopy of date palm is often sparse in comparison to Canary Island date. Their wide use in areas where lethal yellowing disease is resident should also be carefully considered as no variety is known to be resistant.

Scientific Name: *Phoenix reclinata* (fē-niks rek-lin-ah-tah)
Common Name(s): Senegal date, Reclinata palm

Typical Height: 25-30'
Subfamily: Coryphoideae
Tribe: Phoeniceae

Hardiness Zone: 10A-11
Growth Rate: Moderate
Origin: Africa

Landscape Characteristics

Salt Tolerance: Moderate
Drought Tolerance: High
Soil Requirements: Widely adaptable
Light Requirements: High
Nutritional Requirements: Moderate
Uses: Multi-trunked specimen tree
Propagation: Seed, germinating in 2-3 months, division
Human Hazards: Spiny
Major Pest Problems: Palm leaf skeletonizer
Major Disease or Physiological Problems: Ganoderma, stigmina leaf spot, graphiola false smut

Morphology (Identifying Characteristics)

Habit: Clustering, some stems lean or curve forward, each with 25-50 leaves
Trunk or Stem Characteristics: Slender, covered with fiber matting and old leaf stems, eventually clean and ringed with leaf scars
Leaf Type: Pinnately compound, induplicate; with 200-250 leaflets radiating at different angles, the lower ones modified into long spines
Foliage Color: Dark green
Leaf Size: About 15' long; leaflets 1.5' long, 1.75" wide
Petiole: 4' long, armed with leaflet spines
Crownshaft: None
Inflorescence: 3' long, branched
Gender: Separate male and female plants
Flower Color: Cream
Fruit Size: 1/2" long
Fruit Color: Reddish-brown
Irritant: No

Comments: Senegal data palm suckers vigorously and a single plant can consist of more than 20 stems if left unpruned. It hybridizes readily with other date species, and a fair amount of the material in the nursery trade is probably of mixed parentage. It is valued as a specimen plant for accent, but sufficient room is necessary both to allow its natural spread and distance from its dagger-like leaflet spines. Senegal date looks best if trimmed up to reveal the slender, matted trunks. A more open cluster can be achieved by selectively pruning out some of the stems, but may create entry points for the ganoderma fungus.

Scientific Name: *Phoenix roebelenii* (fē-niks rō-bell-én-é-ī)
Common Name(s): Pygmy date palm

Typical Height: 10'
Subfamily: Coryphoideae
Tribe: Phoeniceae

Hardiness Zone: 10A-11
Growth Rate: Slow
Origin: Southeast Asia

Landscape Characteristics

Salt Tolerance: Low
Drought Tolerance: Moderate
Soil Requirements: Widely adaptable
Light Requirements: Moderate, high
Nutritional Requirements: Moderate
Uses: Small tree, container plant
Propagation: Seeds, germinating in 2-3 months
Human Hazards: Spiny
Major Pest Problems: None
Major Disease or Physiological Problems:
Pestalotiopsis, magnesium, manganese and potassium deficiencies, stigmina leaf spot, graphiola false smut

Morphology (Identifying Characteristics)

Habit: Solitary, with a dense crown of 50 or more leaves
Trunk or Stem Characteristics: Relatively slender, often thinnest at base, covered with peg-like leaf bases; mass of aerial roots frequently at base
Leaf Type: Pinnately compound, induplicate, the lowest drooping; leaflets numerous, evenly spaced along rachis, the lower ones spine-like
Foliage Color: Glossy green
Leaf Size: 3-5' long; leaflets 8-15" long, 1/2" wide
Petiole: 2-6" long, armed with leaflet spines
Crownshaft: None
Inflorescence: 1.5' feet long, produced among the leaves, branched
Gender: Separate male and female plants
Flower Color: Cream
Fruit Size: 1/2" long
Fruit Color: Black
Irritant: No

Comments: Pygmy date palm is one of the most widely used date palms in the United States. Though usually single-trunked in nature, multiples are frequently produced in nurseries. This species' small stature, slow rate of growth, ease of culture, and graceful crown have made it a popular accent plant in tropical landscapes. The crown requires occasional trimming of the older leaves. Pygmy date palm is also one of most adaptable dates for container culture, though it does not hold up very well in dimly lit interiors.

Scientific Name: *Phoenix rupicola* (fē-niks roo-pik-ō-lah)
Common Name(s): Cliff date

Typical Height: 25'
Subfamily: Coryphoideae
Tribe: Phoeniceae

Hardiness Zone: 10A-11
Growth Rate: Slow
Origin: India

Landscape Characteristics

Salt Tolerance: Moderate
Drought Tolerance: High
Soil Requirements: Widely adaptable
Light Requirements: High
Nutritional Requirements: Moderate
Uses: Specimen tree
Propagation: Seed, germinating in 2-3 months
Human Hazards: Spiny
Major Pest Problems: None
Major Disease or Physiological Problems: Stigmina leaf spot

Morphology (Identifying Characteristics)

Habit: Solitary; canopy of 30-50 leaves
Trunk or Stem Characteristics: Frequently with only a few leaf bases persisting; swollen near the crown with fiber matting
Leaf Type: Pinnately compound, induplicate, twisted and drooping; with about 200 thin-textured leaflets, the lower leaflets modified into spines
Foliage Color: Bright green
Leaf Size: 10' long; leaflets 1.5' long, 1" wide
Petiole: 3' long, armed with leaflet spines
Crownshaft: None
Inflorescence: 3" long, branched, borne from among the leaves
Gender: Separate male and female plants
Flower Color: White
Fruit Size: 3/4" long
Fruit Color: Yellow, ripening to purple-brown
Irritant: No

Comments: This small but attractive date palm is seeing wider use in the landscape due to its moderate stature and graceful form. The bright green leaflets all lie in one plane, and are softer textured than most dates.

Scientific Name: *Phoenix sylvestris* (fē-niks sil-ves-tris)
Common Name(s): Toddy palm, Wild date palm

Typical Height: 40'
Subfamily: Coryphoideae
Tribe: Phoeniceae

Hardiness Zone: 9-11
Growth Rate: Slow
Origin: India

Landscape Characteristics

Salt Tolerance: Moderate
Drought Tolerance: High
Soil Requirements: Widely adaptable
Light Requirements: High
Nutritional Requirements: Moderate
Uses: Specimen tree
Propagation: Seed, germinating in 2-3 months
Human Hazards: Spiny
Major Pest Problems: None
Major Disease or Physiological Problems: Graphiola false smut

Morphology (Identifying Characteristics)

Habit: Solitary; canopy of 100 leaves
Trunk or Stem Characteristics: Robust, with diamond shaped leaf scars and frequently a skirt of aerial roots at base and persistant leaf bases above
Leaf Type: Pinnately compound, induplicate; lower leaflets modified into spines; 200-250 leaflets arranged in groups of 2 or 3, often criss-crossing
Foliage Color: Blue-green
Leaf Size: 9-12' long; leaflets .5-1.5' long, 1" wide
Petiole: 3' long, armed with leaflet spines
Crownshaft: None
Inflorescence: 2-3' long, much branched; borne from among the leaves
Gender: Separate male and female plants
Flower Color: White
Fruit Size: 1" long
Fruit Color: Orange-yellow, ripening to reddish purple
Irritant: No

Comments: Toddy palm has characteristics in common with the edible date, *P. dactylifera*, and the Canary Island date, *P. canariensis*. It does not sucker and bears shorter leaves than either species. The sap is collected from the cut inflorescences in India and boiled down into sugar (jaggery) or fermented into an alcoholic beverage (toddy). It can be expected that hybrid seed will be formed where it is grown close to other date palm species. Like most of the larger date palms, it makes a durable specimen plant.

Scientific Name: *Pinanga kuhlii* (pin-**nang**-ah cool-ē̄-ī)

Common Name(s): Ivory cane palm

Typical Height: 12'
Subfamily: Arecoideae
Tribe: Areceae

Hardiness Zone: 10B-11
Growth Rate: Moderate
Origin: Java and Sumatra

Landscape Characteristics

Salt Tolerance: Low
Drought Tolerance: Low
Soil Requirements: Widely adaptable
Light Requirements: Moderate
Nutritional Requirements: Moderate
Uses: Foliage plant, specimen shrub
Propagation: Seed, germinating in 2-3 months; division
Human Hazards: None
Major Pest Problems: None
Major Disease or Physiological Problems: None

Morphology (Identifying Characteristics)

Habit: Clustering; each stem with 5-6 leaves
Trunk or Stem Characteristics: Slender, yellowish-green, smooth with light brown ring scars
Leaf Type: Pinnately compound, reduplicate; with a few broad leaflets, the lower ones coming to a curved point, the upper with truncated, toothed tips
Foliage Color: Light green; emerging leaves often pink
Leaf Size: 3-5' long
Petiole: Approximately 1.5' long; unarmed; with brown woolly scales
Crownshaft: Green; inconspicuous
Inflorescence: 1' long from below the crownshaft
Gender: Separate male and female flowers on the same inflorescence
Flower Color: Cream to pink
Fruit Size: 1/2"
Fruit Color: Red
Irritant: No

Comments: This species represents the hardiest member of a large Asian genus of beautiful rain forest understory palms. The attractive color of emerging leaves makes an eye-catching accent in the shade garden, where *P. kuhlii* can be combined with various *Chamaedorea* and *Licuala* species to create a palm understory in the established garden. Sites subject to strong winds, especially cold, drying breezes in winter, should be avoided. The pinangas as a group deserve to be more widely trialed as interior subjects.

Scientific Name: *Pritchardia pacifica* (prit-**chard**-ē-ah pah-**sif**-eh-kah)
Common Name(s): Fiji fan palm

Typical Height: 25'
Subfamily: Coryphoideae
Tribe: Corypheae

Hardiness Zone: 11
Growth Rate: Slow
Origin: Tonga (but introduced by Polynesians to Fiji)

Landscape Characteristics

Salt Tolerance: High
Drought Tolerance: Moderate
Soil Requirements: Widely adaptable
Light Requirements: Moderate, high
Nutritional Requirements: Moderate
Uses: Specimen tree
Propagation: Seed, germinating in 2-3 months
Human Hazards: None
Major Pest Problems: Scales, palm leaf skeletonizer
Major Disease or Physiological Problems: Highly susceptible to lethal yellowing

Morphology (Identifying Characteristics)

Habit: Solitary; canopy of about three dozen leaves
Trunk or Stem Characteristics: Brown, corky, ringed, about 1' in diameter
Leaf Type: Costapalmate, induplicate, cupped upward; divided about 1/4 into many stiff, tapering segments that split at the tip
Foliage Color: Bright green
Leaf Size: 4-8' wide
Petiole: 2.5' feet long, unarmed, waxy, white
Crownshaft: None
Inflorescence: 1-3' long, much branched
Gender: Bisexual flowers
Flower Color: Yellow
Fruit Size: 1/2" diameter
Fruit Color: Blue-black
Irritant: No

Comments: The Pacific fan palms consist of three dozen beautiful species, 2/3 of which are found only on the Hawaiian Islands. Not surprisingly, it is there that most all can be grown to perfection. It is unfortunate that they have proven to be highly susceptible to lethal yellowing disease. Fiji fan palm is well adapted to coastal tropical zones, and performs well in full sun as long as it is never starved for water. Both cold and dry winds will burn the very lovely leaves. Fiji fan palm has a thicker trunk, a denser canopy, and a much shorter flowerstalk than Thurston palm.

Scientific Name: *Pritchardia thurstonii* (prit-**chard**-ē-ah thirs-**tōne**-ē-ī)

Common Name(s): Thurston palm

Typical Height: 25'
Subfamily: Coryphoideae
Tribe: Corypheae

Hardiness Zone: 11'
Growth Rate: Slow
Origin: Fiji

Landscape Characteristics

Salt Tolerance: High
Drought Tolerance: Moderate
Soil Requirements: Widely adaptable
Light Requirements: Moderate, high
Nutritional Requirements: Moderate
Uses: Specimen tree
Propagation: Seed, germinating in 2-3 months
Human Hazards: None
Major Pest Problems: Scales, palm leaf skeletonizer
Major Disease or Physiological Problems: Highly susceptible to lethal yellowing

Morphology (Identifying Characteristics)

Habit: Solitary; canopy of two dozen leaves
Trunk or Stem Characteristics: Brown, vertically fissured, ringed, sometimes slightly swollen at base
Leaf Type: Costapalmate, induplicate, slightly folded upward; divided less than 1/2 into 50 or so stiff, tapering segments that split at the tips
Foliage Color: Bright green
Leaf Size: 4-8' wide
Petiole: 3' feet long, unarmed
Crownshaft: None
Inflorescence: 6-10' long, arching out and down from among the leaves, branched at the tip
Gender: Bisexual flowers
Flower Color: Yellow
Fruit Size: 1/4" diameter
Fruit Color: Red
Irritant: No

Comments: *Pritchardia thurstonii* is well adapted to coastal tropical zones, and performs well on alkaline soils. Though easily cold-damaged, Thurston palm accepts full sun and considerable salt exposure. Young specimens of this beautiful fan palm can be enjoyed for many years as container plants. The high susceptibility to lethal yellowing limits its use to tropical areas not known to harbor the disease.

Scientific Name: *Pseudophoenix sargentii* (sū-dō-fē-niks sar-**gent**-ē-ī)
Common Name(s): Buccaneer palm

Typical Height: 10'
Subfamily: Ceroxyloideae
Tribe: Cyclospatheae

Hardiness Zone: 10B-11
Growth Rate: Slow
Origin: Florida Keys and Caribbean region

Landscape Characteristics

Salt Tolerance: High
Drought Tolerance: High
Soil Requirements: Widely adaptable
Light Requirements: Moderate, high
Nutritional Requirements: Low
Uses: Small tree
Propagation: Seed, germinating in 2-4 months
Human Hazards: None
Major Pest Problems: None
Major Disease or Physiological Problems: None
Cultivars: Several variants have been described on the basis of ultimate height or other minor characteristics

Morphology (Identifying Characteristics)

Habit: Solitary; canopy of 10 leaves
Trunk or Stem Characteristics: Gray-green with light brown rings when young; older trunks dark gray, variably swollen at some point along length
Leaf Type: Pinnately compound, reduplicate, stiff, twisted, with well over a hundred pointed narrow leaflets
Foliage Color: Blue-green
Leaf Size: 9' long; leaflets 2' long, 2" wide
Petiole: 2' feet long, unarmed
Crownshaft: Short, wide, blue-green
Inflorescence: 3' long, from among the leaves
Gender: Separate male and female or bisexual flowers on same inflorescence
Flower Color: Yellow
Fruit Size: 3/4" diameter
Fruit Color: Red
Irritant: No

Comments: This native of the Florida Keys and Caribbean islands is one of the most durable palms for seaside landscaping. Pest-free and highly drought tolerant to boot, the wider use of buccaneer palm has been limited only by its extremely slow rate of growth. No two specimens look alike due to the variable bulging of the trunk.

Other Species: *P. vinifera* (Haiti), the cherry palm, has a thicker trunk and longer leaves on silvery petioles. A wine is made from the sweet juice of the fruit.

Scientific Name: *Ptychosperma elegans* (tĭ-ko-**sper**-mah ell-ē-ganz)
Common Name(s): Solitaire palm, Alexander palm

Typical Height: 20'
Subfamily: Arecoideae
Tribe: Areceae

Hardiness Zone: 10B-11
Growth Rate: Moderate
Origin: Australia

Landscape Characteristics

Salt Tolerance: Low
Drought Tolerance: Moderate
Soil Requirements: Widely adaptable
Light Requirements: Moderate, high
Nutritional Requirements: Moderate
Uses: Specimen tree, interiorscape
Propagation: Seed, germinating in 2-3 months
Human Hazards: None
Major Pest Problems: Scale, palm aphid,
mites (interior)
Major Disease or Physiological Problems:
Ganoderma

Morphology (Identifying Characteristics)

Habit: Solitary, bearing 10-12 leaves in the canopy
Trunk or Stem Characteristics: Slender, gray,
swollen base, ridged leaf scars
Leaf Type: Pinnately compound, reduplicate; with 4-5
dozen pleated leaflets that are bluntly jagged at tip
Foliage Color: Green; leaflets grayish below
Leaf Size: 6-8' long; leaflets 2.5' long, 3-5" wide
Petiole: 1' or less long, with dark brown scaly hairs,
unarmed
Crownshaft: Smooth, waxy
Inflorescence: 2-3 feet long, branched, yellow; borne
below the crownshaft
Gender: Separate male and female flowers on the same
inflorescence
Flower Color: White
Fruit Size: 3/4" long
Fruit Color: Red
Irritant: No

Comments: Solitaire palm is one of the most common palms for tropical landscaping. Its small stature fits well into scaled down residential yards. It is often grown as a multiple specimen, though the species is solitary by nature. It thrives in a site protected from cold and drying winds. Large acclimated specimens are durable interiorscape plants.

Scientific Name: *Ptychosperma macarthurii* (tĭ-ko-**sper**-mah mak-are-**thur**-ē-ī)
Common Name(s): Macarthur palm

Typical Height: 25'
Subfamily: Arecoideae
Tribe: Areceae

Hardiness Zone: 10B-11
Growth Rate: Moderate
Origin: Australia, New Guinea

Landscape Characteristics

Salt Tolerance: Low
Drought Tolerance: Moderate
Soil Requirements: Widely adaptable
Light Requirements: Moderate, high
Nutritional Requirements: Moderate
Uses: Multi-trunked specimen tree, interiorscape
Propagation: Seed, germinating in 2-3 months; division
Human Hazards: None
Major Pest Problems: Palm aphid
Major Disease or Physiological Problems: Sooty mold (accompanying palm aphid infestation usually), ganoderma, phytophthora bud rot
Cultivars: Finer-leafed form said to occur

Morphology (Identifying Characteristics)

Habit: Clustering; each stem bearing 8-10 leaves
Trunk or Stem Characteristics: Very slender, light gray, ridged leaf scars
Leaf Type: Pinnately compound, reduplicate, with 4-5 dozen leaflets bluntly notched at the tip
Foliage Color: Green on both sides
Leaf Size: 3-6' long; leaflets 2.5' long, 2-3" wide
Petiole: 1' long, unarmed
Crownshaft: Smooth, green, waxy especially when young
Inflorescence: 2' long, branched, borne below the crownshaft
Gender: Separate male and female flowers on the same inflorescence
Flower Color: White
Fruit Size: 1/2" long
Fruit Color: Red
Irritant: No

Comments: Macarthur palm is a naturally clumping species, with smaller leaves and skinnier trunks than solitaire palm. It is not used as widely as the latter, but makes an equally fine specimen under the same conditions, though requiring additional space to accommodate its multiple stems.

Scientific Name: *Ravenea glauca* or *rivularis* (rav-en-ē-ah glaw-kah or riv-ū-lair-iss)
Common Name(s): Majesty palm

Typical Height: 15-20' (*glauca*) or 60-80' (*rivularis*)
Subfamily: Ceroxyloideae
Tribe: Ceroxyleae

Hardiness Zone: 10A-11
Growth Rate: Fast
Origin: Madagascar

Landscape Characteristics

Salt Tolerance: Moderate
Drought Tolerance: Moderate
Soil Requirements: Widely adaptable
Light Requirements: Moderate, high
Nutritional Requirements: Moderate to high
Uses: Small specimen tree, interiorscape
Propagation: Seed, germinating in 2-3 months
Human Hazards: None
Major Pest Problems: None
Major Disease or Physiological Problems: None

Morphology (Identifying Characteristics)

Habit: Solitary, robust
Trunk or Stem Characteristics: Gray, swollen at base and gradually tapering upward, attractively ringed
Leaf Type: Pinnately compound, reduplicate, erect at first, then arching, twisted near apex; with numerous, crowded, narrow, ribbed leaflets
Foliage Color: Green
Leaf Size: 6-8' long; leaflets 1.5-2' long, 1" wide
Petiole: Unarmed, fibrous margined
Crownshaft: None
Inflorescence: Short, borne from among the leaves
Gender: Separate male and female plants
Flower Color: White
Fruit Size: 1/2" diameter
Fruit Color: Red
Irritant: No

Comments: The exact identity of the *Ravenea* species known as majesty palm is somewhat uncertain at this writing. Though widely labelled in the nursery industry as *R. rivularis*, a tall growing species, material in cultivation strongly resembles *R. glauca*, a species not known to exceed 20' in height and frequently smaller. Majesty palm is currently finding its widest use as an interior plant. An initial flurry of excitement over its landscape possibilities weakened when it was found to require frequent fertilization or else moderate shade in order to maintain a healthy green color. Majesty palm very quickly reaches about 10' of height, at which point growth slows considerably. Its fast growth rate, interesting trunk, and shade tolerance make it a fine addition to tropical landscapes where it can be situated under the canopy of tall trees to good effect.

Scientific Name: *Rhapidophyllum hystrix* (rah-pid-ō-fill-lum hiss-triks)
Common Name(s): Needle palm

Typical Height: 5'
Subfamily: Coryphoideae
Tribe: Corypheae

Hardiness Zone: 8-10B
Growth Rate: Slow
Origin: Southeastern United States

Landscape Characteristics

Salt Tolerance: Moderate
Drought Tolerance: High (when established)
Soil Requirements: Widely adaptable
Light Requirements: Moderate, high
Nutritional Requirements: Moderate
Uses: Shrub
Propagation: Seed, germinating in 6 months or more; division
Human Hazards: Spiny
Major Pest Problems: None
Major Disease or Physiological Problems: None

Morphology (Identifying Characteristics)

Habit: Clustering, essentially trunkless; stem prostrate or erect; 6-18 leaves
Trunk or Stem Characteristics: Trunkless, fiber-matted crown occasionally elongating to 5'; covered with needle-like fibers from decayed leaf bases
Leaf Type: Palmate, induplicate, divided deeply into 15-20 blunt and jagged tipped segments
Foliage Color: Dark green above, silvery below
Leaf Size: 4' wide; segments 2' long, 3/4" wide
Petiole: 2' long, unarmed
Crownshaft: None
Inflorescence: 1' long, held among the crown fibers and leaves, shortly branched
Gender: Separate male and female plants; occasionally both sexes on same plant
Flower Color: Yellow, purple
Fruit Size: 1" long
Fruit Color: Purple-brown, wooly
Irritant: No

Comments: Though usually found in the understory of rich, hardwood forests, needle palm can be adapted to full sun and makes an interesting specimen plant for accent. Nowhere abundant throughout its broad range, wild populations have been heavily collected in some areas for horticultural production by division of the clumps, largely because the seed is difficult to collect and slow and uneven in germination. Fortunately, nursery seed production is increasing. It is one of the hardier palm species, though growth will be slowest at the northern end of its range.

Scientific Name: *Rhapis excelsa* (ray-piss ek-sell-sa)
Common Name(s): Lady palm

Typical Height: 7'
Subfamily: Coryphoideae
Tribe: Corypheae

Hardiness Zone: 10A-11
Growth Rate: Moderate
Origin: China

Landscape Characteristics

Salt Tolerance: Moderate
Drought Tolerance: Moderate
Soil Requirements: Widely adaptable
Light Requirements: Moderate, low
Nutritional Requirements: Moderate
Uses: Shrub, hedge, specimen plant, interiorscape
Propagation: Seed, germinating over several months with heat; division
Human Hazards: None
Major Pest Problems: Scales, mealybugs, banana moth
Major Disease or Physiological Problems: Iron deficiency; manganese deficiency on alkaline soils
Cultivars: A large number of named variegated forms, propagated by division, are popular in Japan

Morphology (Identifying Characteristics)

Habit: Clustering densely, up to several hundred stems, each with 4-10 leaves
Trunk or Stem Characteristics: Slender, covered with brown matted fiber and protruding leaf bases; eventually black with tan leaf scars
Leaf Type: Palmate, appearing reduplicate, deeply divided into 4-10 wide segments, bluntly toothed at the tip
Foliage Color: Shiny green
Leaf Size: 2.5' wide; segments .5-1" wide
Petiole: 15-18" long, unarmed
Crownshaft: None
Inflorescence: Slender, short, less than 1' long, branched, pinkish; borne from among the upper leaves
Gender: Separate male and female plants; occasionally both sexes on same plant
Flower Color: White
Fruit Size: 1/2" diameter
Fruit Color: White
Irritant: No

Comments: Lady palm is best suited for use in partial shade, where the leaves remain dark, shiny green. In full sun, leaves tend to yellow, and will burn if the roots are allowed to become too dry. Lady palm makes a very effective low screen, but is equally effective as a single specimen shrub (though removal of stems may be necessary in time to keep the plant in bounds). Well-grown, leaves in good condition will clothe the matted stems almost to the base; these can be trimmed up to accent the interesting slender stems. Lady palm has enjoyed great success as an interior plant, and can be maintained in a container for some time. The variegated forms, so popular in Japan, fetch very high prices.

Scientific Name: *Rhapis humilis* (ray-piss hū-mill-is)
Common Name(s): Slender lady palm

Typical Height: 7'
Subfamily: Coryphoideae
Tribe: Corypheae

Hardiness Zone: 9B-11
Growth Rate: Slow
Origin: Southern China, but known only in cultivation

Landscape Characteristics

Salt Tolerance: Moderate
Drought Tolerance: Moderate
Soil Requirements: Widely adaptable
Light Requirements: Moderate, low
Nutritional Requirements: Moderate
Uses: Shrub, hedge, foliage plant
Propagation: Division
Human Hazards: None
Major Pest Problems: Scales, mealybugs
Major Disease or Physiological Problems: None

Morphology (Identifying Characteristics)

Habit: Clustering tightly
Trunk or Stem Characteristics: Slender, covered with very closely woven, light brown fibers and protruding leaf bases; with 4-10 leaves
Leaf Type: Palmate, appearing reduplicate; divided deeply into 15-20 narrow, drooping segments that are almost pointed at the tip
Foliage Color: Green, slightly shiny
Leaf Size: 2-3' wide; segments .5-1" wide
Petiole: 1' long, thin
Crownshaft: None
Inflorescence: 2' long, branched, whitish
Gender: Only male plant known; all material in cultivation divided from this one
Flower Color: White
Fruit Size: Unknown
Fruit Color: Unknown
Irritant: No

Comments: Slender lady palm has smaller stems and leaves than *R. excelsa*, but larger flowerstalks. It is rare as a landscape plant, no doubt due to its slow increase. All material in cultivation is derived from a single male plant known only from cultivation in China. Additional species of *Rhapis*, some quite dwarf, are occasionally offered by nurseries.

Scientific Name: *Roystonea elata* (roy-stŏn-ē-ah ē-lah-tah)
Common Name(s): Florida royal palm

Typical Height: 80'
Subfamily: Arecoideae
Tribe: Areceae

Hardiness Zone: 10A-11
Growth Rate: Moderate
Origin: South Florida

Landscape Characteristics

Salt Tolerance: Moderate
Drought Tolerance: Moderate to low
Soil Requirements: Widely adaptable
Light Requirements: High
Nutritional Requirements: Moderate
Uses: Specimen tree, street tree, border
Propagation: Seed, germinating in 2-3 months, sometimes longer
Human Hazards: Irritant
Major Pest Problems: Royal palm bug
Major Disease or Physiological Problems: Fungal leaf spots, potassium and manganese deficiency (Florida), phytophthora bud rot, ganoderma

Morphology (Identifying Characteristics)

Habit: Solitary, canopy of 12-16 leaves
Trunk or Stem characteristics: Gray, smooth, closely ringed, swollen at base and rarely again higher up
Leaf Type: Pinnately compound, reduplicate; with about 300 leaflets in several ranks giving a plume-like appearance; leaflets without secondary ribs
Foliage Color: Deep green
Leaf Size: 10' long; leaflets 3' long, 2" wide
Petiole: Short, stout, unarmed
Crownshaft: Long, smooth, glossy deep green
Inflorescence: 4' long, loosely branched, the branches somewhat lax
Gender: Separate male and female flowers on the same inflorescence
Flower Color: Yellow
Fruit Size: 1/4" diameter (round)
Fruit Color: Purple
Irritant: Yes

Comments: The Florida royal palm was not widely recognized as a distinct species until L. H. Bailey described it as such in 1949. It is evident from the writings of 18th century naturalist William Bartram that this stately swamp dweller is less widespread in Florida today than it was in the past, whether through habitat destruction, over-collection, or severe winter freezes. It can be distinguished from the Cuban royal only with difficulty. The Florida royal grows taller and usually lacks a bulge in the trunk; has leaflets with inconspicuous or no secondary ribs on either side of the midrib; a longer, more loosely constructed inflorescence; and darker and rounder fruit. The leaflet character is probably the best way to tell them apart. Hybrids between these two closely related species are probably fairly common. Though occurring in cypress swamps in the wild, the Florida royal adapts to well-drained soils readily, though regular irrigation and fertilization on poor, sandy soil is necessary to maintain good growth and color. It will tolerate periodic flooding once established.

Scientific Name: *Roystonea regia* (roy-stōn-ē-ah rē-gē-ah)

Common Name(s): Cuban royal palm

Typical Height: 50-70'
Subfamily: Arecoideae
Tribe: Areceae

Hardiness Zone: 10A-11
Growth Rate: Moderate
Origin: Cuba

Landscape Characteristics

Salt Tolerance: Moderate
Drought Tolerance: Moderate to high
Soil Requirements: Widely adaptable
Light Requirements: High
Nutritional Requirements: Moderate
Uses: Specimen tree, street tree, border
Propagation: Seed, germinating in 2-3 months, sometimes longer
Human Hazards: Irritant
Major Pest Problems: Royal palm bug
Major Disease or Physiological Problems: Fungal leaf spots, potassium deficiency (Florida), ganoderma, phytophthora bud rot

Morphology (Identifying Characteristics)

Habit: Solitary, canopy of about 15 leaves
Trunk or Stem Characteristics: Light gray, smooth, closely ringed, swollen at base and again at middle or just below crownshaft
Leaf Type: Pinnately compound, reduplicate; several hundred multi-ranked leaflets with conspicuous secondary ribs on either side of midrib
Foliage Color: Bright green
Leaf Size: 10' long; leaflets 3' long, 2" wide
Petiole: Short, stout, unarmed
Crownshaft: Long, smooth, deep glossy green
Inflorescence: 3' long, borne just below the crownshaft, tightly branched, the branches straight.
Gender: Separate male and female flowers on the same inflorescence
Flower Color: Yellow
Fruit Size: 1/4" long (oblong)
Fruit Color: Reddish-purple
Irritant: Yes

Comments: The majority of the old, large royal palms in south Florida are specimens of this species, brought from Cuba during the 1930's. Most royal palms sold in nurseries are Cuban, even if they are labeled the Florida royal. The bulging trunk is most characteristic of this species. The Cuban royal occurs natively on upland sites; it is thus likely more drought tolerant than the Florida species. It makes a fine specimen in lawns, however, thriving on the extra irrigation. Royal palms are best avoided when landscaping around modestly sized homes; their stature makes a small house look even smaller. Royal palm bug, which destroys young leaves, can be a persistant problem in Florida, especially after a mild winter. Dimethoate foliar sprays have provided the best control.

Other Species: *R. borinqueana* (Puerto Rico) resembles Cuban royal but has shiny surfaced leaves. *R. oleracea* (Venezuela, southern Caribbean) hold its leaflets in only 1 plane and lacks trunk bulges. *R. princeps* (Jamaica) has a fairly slender trunk and a sparser canopy than most royals.

Scientific Name: *Sabal causiarum* (say-ball caws-ē-are-um)
Common Name(s): Hat palm

Typical Height: 50'
Subfamily: Coryphoideae
Tribe: Corypheae

Hardiness Zone: 9B-11
Growth Rate: Slow
Origin: Puerto Rico

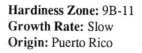

Landscape Characteristics

Salt Tolerance: Moderate
Drought Tolerance: High
Soil Requirements: Widely adaptable
Light Requirements: High
Nutritional Requirements: Low
Uses: Specimen tree
Propagation: Seeds, germinating in 2-3 months
Human Hazards: None
Major Pest Problems: Leaf hoppers
Major Disease or Physiological Problems: Ganoderma

Morphology (Identifying Characteristics)

Habit: Solitary, massive; canopy of about 40 leaves
Trunk or Stem Characteristics: Large diameter; leaf bases shed relatively quickly; gray, smooth and closely ringed
Leaf Type: Costapalmate, induplicate, twisted; divided for about 2/3 of length into numerous segments
Foliage Color: Green
Leaf Size: 6' or more wide; segments 4' long, 2" wide
Petiole: 6' or more long, extending far into leaf blade; unarmed
Crownshaft: None
Inflorescence: Long, much branched, extending past leaves
Gender: Bisexual flowers
Flower Color: White
Fruit Size: 1/3"
Fruit Color: Dark brown to black
Irritant: No

Comments: This relative of the cabbage palm makes an imposing specimen plant on the weight of its massive trunk which achieves nearly 4 feet in diameter. Despite its hardiness (large specimens in Gainesville, Florida attest to a surprising degree of frost resistance for a palm from Puerto Rico), *S. causiarum* has not been widely available from nurseries and is not frequently seen in landscapes, probably because of its slow rate of growth. As with all *Sabal* species, a great deal of underground elaboration of the stem takes place before much top growth is apparent. Even before much trunk development occurs, the canopy of large leaves requires ample room for its spread.

Scientific Name: *Sabal minor* (say-ball my-nore)
Common Name(s): Dwarf palmetto

Typical Height: 6'
Subfamily: Coryphoideae
Tribe: Corypheae

Hardiness Zone: 7-10B
Growth Rate: Slow
Origin: Southeastern United States

Landscape Characteristics

Salt Tolerance: Moderate
Drought Tolerance: High
Soil Requirements: Widely adaptable
Light Requirements: Moderate, low
Nutritional Requirements: Low
Uses: Shrub
Propagation: Seed, germinating in 2-3 months
Human Hazards: None
Major Pest Problems: None
Major Disease or Physiological Problems: Graphiola false smut

Morphology (Identifying Characteristics)

Habit: Solitary, essentially trunkless, with 8-20 leaves
Trunk or Stem Characteristics: Straight or curved underground, very rarely forming a short trunk
Leaf Type: Costapalmate (but shortly), induplicate, flat to slightly folded; divided about halfway into 16-40 stiff, unsplit segments
Foliage Color: Green to blue-green
Leaf Size: 2-5' wide; segments 2' long, 1.75" wide
Petiole: 2-3' long, unarmed
Crownshaft: None
Inflorescence: 3-6' long, erect, rising up above and from among the leaves, much branched
Gender: Bisexual flowers
Flower color: White
Fruit Size: 3/8" diameter
Fruit Color: Black
Irritant: No

Comments: Dwarf palmetto occurs in the understory of woods across a broad swath of the southeastern U.S. It makes an interesting specimen plant in partial shade in areas where few palms could otherwise be grown.

Similar Species: *S. etonia*, the scrub palmetto, occurs only in peninsular Florida. It occurs on drier soils than *S. minor*, and has smaller, deeply folded leaves.

Scientific Name: *Sabal palmetto* (say-ball pahl-met-tō)
Common Name(s): Cabbage palm, sabal palm

Typical Height: 40'
Subfamily: Coryphoideae
Tribe: Corypheae

Hardiness Zone: 8-11
Growth Rate: Slow
Origin: Southeastern United States

Landscape Characteristics	Morphology (Identifying Characteristics)

Salt Tolerance: High
Drought Tolerance: High
Soil Requirements: Widely adaptable
Light Requirements: High
Nutritional Requirements: Low
Uses: Specimen tree
Propagation: Seed, germinating in 2-3 months; stems developed deeply in soil
Human Hazards: None
Major Pest Problems: Palmetto weevils, leaf hoppers
Major Disease or Physiological Problems: Ganoderma, graphiola false smut

Habit: Solitary; canopy of several dozen leaves
Trunk or Stem Characteristics: Gray, smooth; frequently covered with a criss-cross of persistant, split leaf bases
Leaf Type: Costapalmate, induplicate, strongly twisted downward at middle; divided to about 1/2 into numerous segments, some stiff, some drooping
Foliage Color: Dull green
Leaf Size: To 6' wide; segments 3-4' long, 2-3" wide
Petiole: 4-6' long, unarmed; leaf base split
Crownshaft: None
Inflorescence: 6-8' long, openly branched, borne among the leaves
Gender: Bisexual flowers
Flower Color: White
Fruit Size: 1/2" diameter
Fruit Color: Black
Irritant: No

Comments: The state tree of both Florida and South Carolina, cabbage palm is one of the most common native palms in the United States, and is widely used for landscaping, adapting well to many different soils and situations. Trees are harvested from wild stands at a fraction of the cost of a similarly sized nursery-grown palm. Sabal palms transplant well, but cut roots do not branch as they do in all other palms examined, and the palm must therefore produce new roots from the base of the trunk. It has been found that removing all leaves from these palms at the time of digging increases survival rate after installation. Cabbage palms vary in the persistence of their leaf bases. Some remain "booted" for many years; others shed the leaf bases fairly quickly.

Similar Species: *S. mexicana*, occurring along the Rio Grande valley in Texas and Mexico, is similar to *S. palmetto*, but has a slightly more robust trunk. It is cultivated primarily in south Texas.

Scientific Name: *Serenoa repens* (sayr-ren-ō-ah rep-ens)
Common Name(s): Saw palmetto

Typical Height: 3-6'
Subfamily: Coryphoideae
Tribe: Corypheae

Hardiness Zone: 8-11
Growth Rate: Slow
Origin: Southeastern United States

Green form.

Blue-green form.

Landscape Characteristics

Salt Tolerance: High
Drought Tolerance: High
Soil Requirements: Widely adaptable
Light Requirements: Moderate, high
Nutritional Requirements: Low
Uses: Shrub, groundcover
Propagation: Seed, germinating in several months
Human Hazards: Spiny
Major Pest Problems: Palmetto weevils
Major Disease or Physiological Problems: Ganoderma
Cultivars: Blue-green leaved forms occur naturally along the southern east coast of Florida

Morphology (Identifying Characteristics)

Habit: Clumping, essentially trunkless; each stem with 12-30 leaves
Trunk or Stem characteristics: Mostly underground, sometimes growing prostrate along the ground or rarely erect; covered with leaf bases and fiber
Leaf Type: Palmate, induplicate, slightly folded, stiff; divided deeply into several dozen segments that split at the tip
Foliage Color: Green or blue-green, waxy
Leaf Size: 3-4' wide; segments about 2' long, 1" wide
Petiole: 3-5' long, saw-toothed at margins
Crownshaft: None
Inflorescence: 2-3' long, much-branched, borne among the leaves
Gender: Bisexual flowers
Flower Color: White
Fruit Size: 1" long
Fruit Color: Blue black
Irritant: No, but smell like rancid butter as they age

Comments: Saw palmetto forms a conspicuous ground cover in pinelands along the southern coastal plain. With the growing interest in native plants, nursery production of saw palmetto has steadily increased. The blue-green forms are particularly prized for naturalistic landscapes. Large specimens do not transplant easily, and the plants are best established from containers. The fruits are the source of a kidney medicine widely used in Mexico (but not FDA approved in the United States) and are often sold dry as an herbal remedy in health food stores. The flowers produce a fine honey, and beekeepers frequently move hives onto the pinelands when the saw palmettos begin to flower.

Scientific Name: *Syagrus romanzoffiana* (sigh-**ag**-russ rōme-an-zoff-ē-**ann**-um)
Common Name(s): Queen palm, Cocos plumosa

Typical Height: 40'
Subfamily: Arecoideae
Tribe: Cocoeae

Hardiness Zone: 10A-11
Growth Rate: Fast
Origin: Southern Brazil to Argentina

Landscape Characteristics

Salt Tolerance: Moderate
Drought Tolerance: Moderate
Soil Requirements: Slightly acid best, but fairly adaptable
Light Requirements: Moderate, high
Nutritional Requiments: High
Uses: Specimen tree
Propagation: Seed, germinating in 3-6 months
Human Hazards: Allergy to pollen
Major Pest Problems: None
Major Disease or Physiological Problems: Manganese and potassium deficiency, ganoderma, gliocladium blight (California), phytophthora bud rot
Cultivars: 'Robusta' or 'Australis' sometimes ascribed to particularly robust forms

Morphology (Identifying Characteristics)

Habit: Solitary; canopy of 15 or so leaves
Trunk or Stem characteristics: Gray, smooth, sometimes bulging at some point, widely spaced rings
Leaf Type: Pinnately compound, reduplicate, arching; with several hundred many ranked, drooping leaflets in groups of 2-7
Foliage Color: Dark green
Leaf Size: 10-15' long; leaflets 3' long, 1.75" wide
Petiole: 6' long, fibrous margined on the broad, sheathing base; unarmed
Crownshaft: None
Inflorescence: 4-8' long, with conspicuous bract, borne from among the leaves, branched densely, the branches pendulous
Gender: Separate male and female flowers on the same inflorescence
Flower Color: White
Fruit Size: 1.25" diameter
Fruit Color: Yellow to orange
Irritant: No

Comments: Queen palm has become the standard urban palm throughout south Florida, and is grown in southern California where supplementary water can be provided. The species is somewhat weak-rooted and can topple in strong winds. It transplants easily, grows quickly, and is bothered by few pests or diseases. The canopy of large leaves is very graceful in appearance. "Frizzletop," caused by manganese deficiency, is frequently a problem if fertilizer is not provided periodically and especially on alkaline soils. Young specimens often carry widely-spaced leaves almost to the base of the stem. The queen palm produces copious quantities of fruit which some consider messy.

Other Species: *S. amara* (Lesser Antilles), the overtop palm, is a salt tolerant species with a tall slender trunk and a broad canopy of coconut-like leaves. *S. cornonata* (Brazil), the licury palm, has a thick trunk covered with conspicuous leaf bases arranged in eye-catching vertical or spiral rows. Neither are as fast-growing as queen palm.

Scientific Name: *Syagrus schizophylla* (sigh-ag-russ skiz-ō-fill-ah)
Common Name(s): Arikury palm

Typical Height: 15'
Subfamily: Arecoideae
Tribe: Cocoeae

Hardiness Zone: 10A-11
Growth Rate: Slow
Origin: Brazil

Landscape Characteristics

Salt Tolerance: Moderate
Drought Tolerance: High
Soil Requirements: Widely adaptable
Light Requirements: Moderate, high
Nutritional Requirements: Moderate
Uses: Small tree, interiorscape
Propagation: Seed, germinating in 1-2 months
Human Hazards: Spiny
Major Pest Problems: None
Major Disease or Physiological Problems: Slightly susceptible to lethal yellowing; ganoderma

Morphology (Identifying Characteristics)

Habit: Solitary; canopy of several dozen crowded leaves
Trunk or Stem Characteristics: Dark brown, clothed with old leaf stem bases in distinctive spiral pattern with fiber in between
Leaf Type: Pinnately compound, reduplicate, arching; with about 80 pointed, lax leaflets in one plane
Foliage Color: Green
Leaf Size: 6'long; leaflets 2' long, 1" wide
Petiole: 2-3' long, narrow, purple-black, with spiny fibers at the margins
Crownshaft: None
Inflorescence: 2-3' long, borne from among the lower leaves, pendulous, once-branched
Gender: Separate male and female flowers on the same inflorescence
Flower Color: White
Fruit Size: 1" diameter
Fruit Color: Orange
Irritant: No; edible (but insipid)

Comments: The arikury palm grows well in and may even prefer partial shade. Its small stature and interesting leaf stem base pattern on the trunk make it a striking specimen plant that will not outgrow its situation. Young plants are very attractive and are starting to be offered as indoor plants.

Scientific Name: *Thrinax morrisii* (thrī-naks more-iss-ē-i)
Common Name(s): Key thatch palm, Peaberry palm

Typical Height: 20' but often smaller
Subfamily: Coryphoideae
Tribe: Corypheae

Hardiness Zone: 10B-11
Growth Rate: Slow
Origin: Florida Keys and Caribbean islands

Landscape Characteristics

Salt Tolerance: High
Drought Tolerance: High
Soil Requirements: Widely adaptable, but high tolerance of alkalinity
Light Requirements: Moderate, high
Nutritional Requirements: Low
Uses: Small tree
Propagation: Seed, germinating in 2-3 months
Human Hazards: None
Major Pest Problems: None
Major Disease or Physiological Problems: None
Cultivars: None, but individuals vary in the degree of silver wax on the leaf underside

Morphology (Identifying Characteristics)

Habit: Solitary; canopy of 20-30 leaves
Trunk or Stem Characteristics: Slender, gray, inconspicuously ringed; split leaf bases and unruly fiber persist for some time; root mass at swollen base
Leaf Type: Palmate, induplicate, irregularly folded; split about halfway into 40-50 segments, some lax, others stiff; rounded hastula
Foliage Color: Shiny green above, silver below
Leaf Size: 4-5' wide; segments 3' long, 1.5-2" wide
Petiole: 4-6' long, narrow, unarmed
Crownshaft: None
Inflorescence: 3-6' long, openly branched; erect at first, than arching or drooping
Gender: Bisexual flowers
Flower color: White
Fruit Size: 1/4" diameter
Fruit color: White
Irritant: No

Comments: This beautiful thatch palm is perfectly adapted to alkaline sands or limestone outcrops and takes full coastal exposure as well. Inland from the shore, it is just as amenable to garden use, but should be situated where drainage is fast. The nicest specimens have leaves deeply overlaid with silver on the underside. These catch the bright sun as they wave in a sea breeze. Keys thatch palm (and all other *Thrinax*) can be separated from silver palms (*Coccothrinax* spp.) by the split leaf bases, very folded leaves, and uniformly white fruits.

Scientific Name: *Thrinax radiata* (thrī-naks rā-dē-ah-tah)
Common Name(s): Florida thatch palm

Typical Height: 20'
Subfamily: Coryphoideae
Tribe: Corypheae

Hardiness Zone: 10B-11
Growth Rate: Slow
Origin: Southernmost Florida and Caribbean region

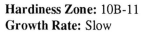

Landscape Characteristics

Salt Tolerance: High
Drought Tolerance: High
Soil Requirements: Widely adaptable, but particularly adapted to alkaline soils
Light Requirements: Moderate, high
Nutritional Requirements: Low
Uses: Small tree
Propagation: Seed, germinating in 2-3 months
Human Hazards: None
Major Pest Problems: None
Major Disease or Physiological Problems: None

Morphology (Identifying Characteristics)

Habit: Solitary; canopy of 12-20 leaves
Trunk or Stem Characteristics: Slender, gray, indistinctly ringed, swollen at base; covered with split leaf bases and fiber in upper portions
Leaf Type: Palmate, induplicate, circular, slightly folded; divided about halfway into 30-50 segments that are split at the tips; pointed hastula
Foliage Color: Green with yellow ribs above; yellowish-green below
Leaf Size: 4-5' wide; segments 2.5' long, 2" wide
Petiole: 2-3' long, unarmed; base split, fibrous, reddish
Crownshaft: None
Inflorescence: 3-4' long, erect to arching; borne from among the leaves
Gender: Bisexual flowers
Flower Color: White
Fruit Size: 1/4" diameter
Fruit Color: White
Irritant: No

Comments: Florida thatch palm is a carefree if slow-growing small palm with excellent seaside and alkali tolerance. Best in full sun, it will tolerate partial shade as well. It has proven resistant to frost and could be tried with protection in zone 10A.

Similar Species: *T. parviflora* (Jamaica), the broom thatch palm, has a smooth trunk and a denser canopy than Florida thatch palm.

Scientific Name: *Trachycarpus fortunei* (trā-kē-car-puss for-**tune**-ē-ī)
Common Name(s): Windmill palm, Chusan, Chinese windmill palm

Typical Height: 25' (but can grow as tall as 40')
Subfamily: Coryphoideae
Tribe: Corypheae

Hardiness Zone: 8-10B
Growth Rate: Slow
Origin: China

Landscape Characteristics

Salt Tolerance: Moderate
Drought Tolerance: High
Soil Requirements: Widely adaptable
Light Requirements: Moderate, high
Nutritional Requirements: Moderate
Uses: Small tree
Propagation: Seed, germinating in 2 months
Human Hazards: Slightly spiny
Major Pest Problems: None
Major Disease or Physiological Problems: Moderately susceptible to lethal yellowing, phytophthora bud rot

Morphology (Identifying Characteristics)

Habit: Solitary; canopy of 20-30 leaves
Trunk or Stem Characteristics: Slender, covered with unruly dark brown fibers that age to gray and protruding leaf bases
Leaf Type: Palmate, induplicate; divided almost to the base into about 3 dozen stiff or drooping segments that shortly split at their tips
Foliage Color: Dark green above, silvery below
Leaf Size: 2-3' wide; segments 1.5-2' long, 1" wide
Petiole: 1.5' long, bluntly toothed on the margins
Crownshaft: None
Inflorescence: 1.5' long, densely branched
Gender: Separate male and female plants
Flower Color: Yellow, fragrant
Fruit Size: 1/2" long
Fruit Color: Blue
Irritant: No

Comments: Windmill palm is one of the hardiest palms in cultivation, capable of withstanding fairly severe freezes with no damage. In its native habitat, it may even receive a light winter snow cover. Hot tropical climates are not to this species' liking, and specimens tend to be short-lived in those areas. It has also proven at least moderately susceptible to lethal yellowing. Windmill palm is most useful for providing a tropical accent in warm temperate zones, and grows well in cool summer areas such as coastal California and parts of the British Isles that receive the effects of the Gulf Stream. It is tolerant of partial shade.

Other Species: *T. martianus* (Eastern Himalayas) grows slightly taller than windmill palm, and has a slimmer trunk that tends to be clean of fiber and leaf bases in its lower portions.

Scientific Name: *Trithrinax acanthocoma* (trī-thrī-aks   ah-kan-thō-kŏm-ah)
Common Name(s): Spiny fiber palm

Typical Height: 15'
Subfamily: Coryphoideae
Tribe: Corypheae

Hardiness Zone: 9-11
Growth Rate: Slow
Origin: Southern Brazil

Landscape Characteristics

Salt Tolerance: Moderate
Drought Tolerance: High
Soil Requirements: Widely adaptable
Light Requirements: High
Nutritional Requirements: Low
Uses: Specimen plant, small tree
Propagation: Seed, germinating in 3 or more months
Human Hazards: Spiny
Major Pest Problems: None
Major Disease or Physiological Problems:
Phytophthora bud rot

Morphology (Identifying Characteristics)

Habit: Solitary; canopy of about 20 leaves
Trunk or Stem Characteristics: Thick, covered with old leaf bases and spiny brown fibers
Leaf Type: Palmate, induplicate; divided about halfway into several dozen broad, pointed segments that split at their tips and sometimes droop
Foliage Color: Deep green above, whitish below
Leaf Size: 3-4' feet wide; segments 2' long, 2" wide
Petiole: 3' long, unarmed
Crownshaft: None
Inflorescence: 3-4' long, much-branched, the branches thick and white
Gender: Bisexual flowers
Flower Color: White
Fruit Size: 1" diameter
Fruit Color: Yellow-green to white
Irritant: No

Comments: About five species comprise the genus *Trithrinax*. They have not been widely cultivated, but deserve to be tried more widely since they appear reasonably hardy. Spiny fiber palm makes a striking specimen plant as long as contact with the fibrous spines on the trunk can be avoided. The crown of leaves has a very pleasing symmetrical aspect that fits well into a formal landscape design. It is extremely well-adapted to alkaline soils.

Other Species: *T. brasiliensis* (Brazil to Paraguay) flowers when quite small. The white inflorescences and flowers, appearing several at a time, are fairly showy. *T. campestris* (Argentina), is a clumping species with unusual leaves that are woolly white on the upper side and glossy green below.

Scientific Name: *Veitchia arecina* (vē-chē-ah ar-ē-sē-nah)
Common Name(s): Arecina palm

Typical Height: 25'
Subfamily: Arecoideae
Tribe: Areceae

Hardiness Zone: 10B-11
Growth Rate: Fast
Origin: Vanuatu (formerly New Hebrides Islands)

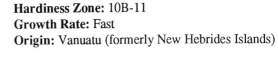

Landscape Characteristics

Salt Tolerance: Moderate
Drought Tolerance: Moderate
Soil Requirements: Widely adaptable
Light Requirements: Moderate, high
Nutritional Requirements: Moderate
Uses: Specimen tree
Propagation: Seed, germinating in 1-2 months
Human Hazards: None
Major Pest Problems: None
Major Disease or Physiological Problems: Slight
susceptibility to lethal yellowing

Morphology (Identifying Characteristics)

Habit: Solitary; canopy of 8-10 leaves
Trunk or Stem Characteristics: Slender, gray, rough,
closely ringed, slightly swollen at base
Leaf Type: Pinnately compound, reduplicate, arching,
drooping slightly with age; with about 90 drooping
leaflets, toothed at their tips
Foliage Color: Green, leaflet scales absent on
underside
Leaf Size: About 8' long; leaflets 2' long, 3" wide
Petiole: About 1' long, whitish-green
Crownshaft: Whitish green, with brown scales near top
Inflorescence: About 3' long, much branched, smooth,
whitish
Gender: Separate male and female flowers on the same
inflorescence
Flower Color: Greenish-white
Fruit Size: 1-2" long
Fruit Color: Red
Irritant: No

Comments: Arecina palm is among the lesser statured *Veitchia* species, useful as a specimen tree in small spaces, yet resistant to lethal yellowing disease. With the exception of manila palm, the *Veitchia* species treated here are similar in general appearance, differing primarily in ultimate size and by a few relatively inconspicuous foliage characters. All are fine specimen palms for moist tropical landscapes, and function well in group plantings. They are fast growing, attractive in fruit, and generally neat in appearance. Cold traps should be avoided when situating these palms in the landscape. Drying winds will also burn the leaves.

Scientific Name: *Veitchia joannis* (vē-chē-ah jō-ann-iss)

Common Name(s): Joannis palm

Typical Height: 60'
Subfamily: Arecoideae
Tribe: Areceae

Hardiness Zone: 10B-11
Growth Rate: Fast
Origin: Fiji

Landscape Characteristics

Salt Tolerance: Moderate
Drought Tolerance: Moderate
Soil Requirements: Widely adaptable
Light Requirements: Moderate, high
Nutritional Requirements: Moderate
Uses: Specimen tree
Propagation: Seed, germinating in 1-2 months
Human Hazards: None
Major Pest Problems: None
Major Disease or Physiological Problems: None

Morphology (Identifying Characteristics)

Habit: Solitary; canopy of 8-10 leaves
Trunk or Stem Characteristics: Slender, gray-brown, widely ringed, slightly swollen at base
Leaf Type: Pinnately compound, reduplicate, drooping downward; with 140-160 obliquely tipped leaflets at a 45° angle from the rachis
Foliage Color: Dark green; leaflets lack scales on underside
Leaf Size: 6-10' long; leaflets 1-2.5' long, 2" wide
Petiole: Short, unarmed
Crownshaft: Grayish-green, with pale brown woolly scales at top
Inflorescence: 2-3' long, much branched, borne below the crownshaft, somewhat pendulous, with soft greenish white hairs on ultimate branchlets
Gender: Separate male and female flowers on the same inflorescence
Flower Color: Greenish-white
Fruit Size: 1-1.5" long
Fruit Color: Red
Irritant: No

Comments: Joannis palm can be distinguished from the other similar veitchias by the habit of the leaves which droop much below the horizontal as they age. It is one of the taller growing veitchias commonly cultivated. Joannis palm makes a beautiful specimen plant in warm tropical regions and lend itself well to grove plantings. The red fruits, borne in quantity over a fairly long period, are also highly ornamental. The leaves can burn if exposed to cold or drying winds.

Scientific Name: *Veitchia macdanielsii* (vē-chē-ah mak-**dan**-yels-ē-ī)

Common Name(s): Sunshine palm

Typical Height: 50'
Subfamily: Arecoideae
Tribe: Areceae

Hardiness Zone: 10B-11
Growth Rate: Fast
Origin: Vanuatu (formerly the New Hebrides Islands)

Landscape Characteristics

Salt Tolerance: Moderate
Drought Tolerance: Moderate
Soil Requirements: Widely adaptable
Light Requirements: Moderate, high
Nutritional Requirements: Moderate
Uses: Specimen tree
Propagation: Seed, germinating in 1-2 months
Human Hazards: None
Major Pest Problems: None
Major Disease or Physiological Problems: None

Morphology (Identifying Characteristics)

Habit: Solitary; compact canopy of 8-10 leaves
Trunk or Stem characteristics: Slender, whitish gray, widely ringed, swollen at base
Leaf Type: Pinnately compound, reduplicate, spreading but held above the horizontal; with 70 or so broad, obliquely tipped leaflets
Foliage Color: Green; leaflets with scales on underside near midrib
Leaf Size: 8-9' long; leaflets 1.5' long, 4" wide
Petiole: Short, gray-green, unarmed
Crownshaft: Whitish-green, black woolly scales near top
Inflorescence: 4' long, much branched, borne below the crownshaft
Gender: Separate male and female flowers on the same inflorescence
Flower Color: White
Fruit Size: 1.25" long
Fruit Color: Red
Irritant: No

Comments: Sunshine palm has the most compact canopy of the taller growing veitchia palms. The leaves have a relatively small number of rather broad leaflets. The leaves are almost always slightly inclined above the horizontal.

<h2 style="text-align:center">Scientific Name: Veitchia merrillii (vē-chē-ah mer-ill-ē-ī)</h2>
<h2 style="text-align:center">Common Name(s): Manila palm, Adonidia, Christmas palm</h2>

Typical Height: 15' (to 25')
Subfamily: Arecoideae
Tribe: Areceae

Hardiness Zone: 10B-11
Growth Rate: Moderate
Origin: Philippines

Landscape Characteristics

Salt Tolerance: Moderate
Drought Tolerance: Moderate
Soil Requirements: Widely adaptable
Light Requirements: Moderate, high
Nutritional Requirements: Moderate
Uses: Small specimen tree, large containers, interior-scape
Propagation: Seed, germinating in 1-2 months
Human Hazards: None
Major Pest Problems: None
Major Disease or Physiological Problems: Highly susceptible to lethal yellowing ("veitchia decline")

Morphology (Identifying Characteristics)

Habit: Solitary, canopy of 9-15 leaves
Trunk or Stem characteristics: Slender, dark to light gray, smooth or slightly rough, closely ringed, swollen at base
Leaf Type: Pinnately compound, reduplicate, stiffly arching; with 100 jagged tipped leaflets held in several planes near base and in a "V" above
Foliage Color: Bright green
Leaf Size: 4-6' long; leaflets 1.5-2.5' long, 2" wide
Petiole: Short, 5-8" long, smooth, unarmed
Crownshaft: Short and thick, bright green with fine white scales
Inflorescence: About 2' long, borne below the crownshaft, much-branched, white
Gender: Separate male and female flowers on the same inflorescence
Flower Color: White
Fruit Size: 1.25" long
Fruit Color: Red, glossy
Irritant: No

Comments: Though not as fast growing as the other *Veitchia* species in cultivation, adonidia has long been the most popular, due to its neat and formal appearance and since its small size lends itself to wide use, even in the smallest residential yards. It has also been grown for interior use, having less a tendency to stretch under shade conditions than the faster and taller growing species. The showy fruit display of this palm coincides with Christmas time. Unfortunately, high susceptibility to lethal yellowing now limits its use to areas free of the disease.

Scientific Name: *Veitchia montgomeryana* (vē-chē-ah mont-gom-er-ē-**ann**-ah)
Common Name(s): Montgomery palm

Typical Height: 25-35'
Subfamily: Arecoideae
Tribe: Areceae

Hardiness Zone: 10B-11
Growth Rate: Fast
Origin: Vanuatu (formerly the New Hebrides Islands)

Landscape Characteristics

Salt Tolerance: Moderate
Drought Tolerance: Moderate
Soil Requirements: Widely adaptable
Light Requirements: Moderate, high
Nutritional Requirements: Moderate
Uses: Specimen tree
Propagation: Seed, germinating in 1-2 months
Human Hazards: None
Major Pest Problems: None
Major Disease or Physiological Problems: Slightly susceptible to lethal yellowing

Morphology (Identifying Characteristics)

Habit: Solitary; canopy of 8-10 leaves
Trunk or Stem Characteristics: Slender, gray (often green for some distance below the crownshaft), widely ringed, slightly swollen at base
Leaf Type: Pinnately compound, reduplicate, held at the horizontal; with 120-140 evenly spaced, stiff narrow tipped leaflets that taper at both ends
Foliage Color: Dark green, whitish scales on underside of leaflets near midrib
Leaf Size: 10' long; leaflets 1.5" long, 3" wide
Petiole: About 1' long, gray-green
Crownshaft: Bright green with fine, gray to rust-colored scales; patches of black woolly scales at top
Inflorescence: 2.5-3' long, thick, much branched
Gender: Separate male and female flowers on the same inflorescence
Flower Color: White
Fruit Size: 1.5" long
Fruit Color: Red
Irritant: No

Comments: Formerly lumped with *V. joannis*, the Montgomery palm is similar in appearance but does not get as tall nor drop its leaves below a horizontal position. The scales on the leaf stem bases are considerably darker than in that species. Montgomery palm has become increasingly popular for landscaping, despite its slight susceptibilty to lethal yellowing. Collection for palm heart is threatening its existence in the wild.

Scientific Name: *Veitchia winin* (vē-chē-ah win-in)
Common Name(s): Winin palm

Typical Height: 50'
Subfamily: Arecoideae
Tribe: Areceae

Hardiness Zone: 10B-11
Growth Rate: Fast
Origin: Vanuatu (formerly the New Hebrides Islands)

Landscape Characteristics

Salt Tolerance: Moderate
Drought Tolerance: High
Soil Requirements: Widely adaptable
Light Requirements: Moderate, high
Nutritional Requirements: Moderate
Uses: Specimen tree
Propagation: Seed, germinating in 1-2 months
Human Hazards: None
Major Pest Problems: None
Major Disease or Physiological Problems: None

Morphology (Identifying Characteristics)

Habit: Solitary; canopy of 8-10 leaves
Trunk or Stem Characteristics: Grayish brown, slender, swollen at base, ringed
Leaf Type: Pinnately compound, reduplicate, older leaves slightly drooping; about 120 evenly spaced leaflets broadest at the middle and toothed at tip
Foliage Color: Green, whitish scales on leaflet underside near midrib
Leaf Size: 12-15' long; leaflets 2' long, 3" wide
Petiole: About 1' long, reddish-brown
Crownshaft: Long; pale green with powdery white scales
Inflorescence: 2' long, borne below crownshaft, white, branched; fiber tufts present at scar after flower stem falls off
Gender: Separate male and female flowers on same inflorescence
Flower Color: White
Fruit Size: 1/2" long
Fruit Color: Red
Irritant: No

Comments: Similar in appearance to both joannis and montgomery palm, winin palm has a somewhat more open canopy and long leaves that only droop slightly below the horizontal as they age. The leaf stems are heavily marked with brownish scales.

Scientific Name: *Washingtonia filifera* (wash-ing-tōn-e-ah fill-if-er-ah)
Common Name(s): Desert fan palm, California fan palm, Petticoat palm

Typical Height: 50'
Subfamily: Coryphoideae
Tribe: Corypheae

Hardiness Zone: 8-11
Growth Rate: Moderate
Origin: California, Arizona

Landscape Characteristics

Salt Tolerance: Moderate
Drought Tolerance: High
Soil Requirements: Widely adaptable
Light Requirements: High
Nutritional Requirements: Moderate
Uses: Specimen tree, street tree
Propagation: Seed, germinating in 6 weeks to 2 months
Human Hazards: Spiny
Major Pest Problems: None
Major Disease or Physiological Problems: Phytophthora bud rot, pestalotiopsis, diamond scale fungus

Morphology (Identifying Characteristics)

Habit: Solitary, robust; canopy of several dozen leaves
Trunk or Stem Characteristics: Brown, fairly thick, not swollen at base, closely ringed, fissured; clothed with shag of dead leaves for many years
Leaf Type: Costapalmate, induplicate; divided at least halfway into 50-70 pointed segments that bend and split at the tips with threads inbetween
Foliage Color: Grayish-green
Leaf Size: 6-7' wide; segments 3-4' long, 2-3" wide
Petiole: 4-6' long, green, toothed at margin
Crownshaft: None
Inflorescence: 9-15' long, branched, hanging down from among the leaves
Gender: Bisexual flowers
Flower Color: White
Fruit Size: 3/8" diameter
Fruit Color: Brownish black
Irritant: No

Comments: The California fan palm does not get as tall as the Mexican *Washingtonia*, nor grow as tall, but the trunk is considerably thicker. In many respects, it makes a more attractive specimen, especially with age. Mixed plantings are not uncommon in California, though probably unintentional, and hybrids between both species are common.

Scientific Name: *Washingtonia robusta* (wash-ing-tōn-ē-ah rō-**buss**-tah)
Common Name(s): Washington palm, Mexican fan palm

Typical Height: 70-100'
Subfamily: Coryphoideae
Tribe: Corypheae

Hardiness Zone: 8-11
Growth Rate: Fast
Origin: Mexico

Landscape Characteristics

Salt Tolerance: Moderate
Drought Tolerance: High
Soil Requirements: Widely adaptable
Light Requirements: High
Nutritional Requirements: Moderate
Uses: Specimen tree, street tree
Propagation: Seed, germinating readily in 6 weeks to 2 months
Human Hazards: Spiny
Major Pest Problems: Palmetto weevils, scales
Major Disease or Physiological Problems: Phytophthora bud rot, graphiola false smut, ganoderma, pestalotiopsis

Morphology (Identifying Characteristics)

Habit: Solitary; canopy of about 30 leaves
Trunk or Stem Characteristics: Pale gray, closely ringed, fissured, swollen at base; often covered for years with a long shag of dead leaves
Leaf Type: Costapalmate, induplicate; divided halfway or more into pointed, ribbed, drooping segments with white threads in between on younger plants
Foliage Color: Bright green
Leaf Size: 4-6' wide; segments 2-4' long; 1.5" wide
Petiole: 3-4' long, orange; sharp teeth on margin; base reddish-brown and split
Crownshaft: None
Inflorescence: 8-12' long, branched, borne from among the leaf bases and pendulous
Gender: Bisexual flowers
Flower color: Off-white
Fruit Size: 3/8" diameter
Fruit Color: Brownish black
Irritant: No

Comments: Mexican fan palm has traditionally been more widely grown in Florida than its close relative, the California washington palm, probably because of its faster growth rate. Hybrids between the two species occur, and many specimens in landscapes in both Florida and California are likely of mixed ancestry. Though a desert palm, the species lives nearby permanent surface or sub-surface water, and fastest growth occurs with periodic irrigation, especially during establishment. In humid, subtropical climates, over-watering can lead to root and bud rots. With age, Mexican fan palm loses some of its appeal as the trunk tapers and thins. In Florida, lightning commonly ends the landscape life of this palm as soon as it begins to tower over surrounding vegetation. It is the tallest growing of the hardier palms.

Scientific Name: *Wodyetia bifurcata* (wŏd-yeh-tē-ah bĭ-fer-**cah**-tah)
Common Name(s): Foxtail palm

Typical Height: 30'
Subfamily: Arecoideae
Tribe: Areceae

Hardiness Zone: 10A-11
Growth Rate: Fast
Origin: Northern Australia

Landscape Characteristics

Salt Tolerance: Moderate
Drought Tolerance: Moderate
Soil Requirements: Widely adaptable
Light Requirements: Moderate, high
Nutritional Requirements: Moderate
Uses: Specimen tree
Propagation: Seed, germinating in 2-3 months
Human Hazards: None
Major Pest Problems: None
Major Disease or Physiological Problems: Leaf spots with overhead watering

Morphology (Identifying Characteristics)

Habit: Solitary; canopy of 8-10 leaves
Trunk or Stem Characteristics: Slender, gray, swollen at base, ringed with leaf scars
Leaf Type: Pinnately compound, reduplicate, arching; several hundred fishtail leaflets attached in several ranks; marginal reins frequent
Foliage Color: Deep green; silvery on underside
Leaf Size: 8-10' long; leaflets about 6" long, 2" wide (widest point at tip)
Petiole: .5-1' long, whitish green, with brown scales
Crownshaft: Narrow, green with whitish waxy scales; leaf sheaths with dark brown scales at top
Inflorescence: Branched, borne below the crownshaft, green
Gender: Separate male and female flowers on the same inflorescence
Flower Color: White
Fruit Size: 2" long
Fruit Color: Red
Irritant: No

Comments: The foxtail palm, little known before the last few years, has taken the palm world by storm. There is currently an unprecedented demand in the nursery industry for seed, and this attractive Australian species will likely become one of the most popular items for landscaping in moist tropical and subtropical areas. The common name is derived from the very full appearance of the leaves, formed by the circular arrangement of the leaflets around the rachis. Foxtail palm is very fast-growing, and appears adaptable to a broad range of soil conditions. Young plants can be afflicted by leaf spot fungi, though not consistently; this seems to be aggravated by frequent overhead irrigation. Foxtail palm takes full sun even at a young age.

Scientific Name: *Zombia antillarum* (zom-bē-ah an-till-are-um)
Common Name(s): Zombie palm

Typical Height: 15'
Subfamily: Coryphoideae
Tribe: Corypheae

Hardiness Zone: 10B-11
Growth Rate: Slow
Origin: Hispaniola

Salt Tolerance: High
Drought Tolerance: High
Soil Requirements: Widely adaptable
Light Requirements: Moderate, high
Nutritional Requirements: Low
Uses: Specimen plant, shrub
Propagation: Seed, germinating in 2 months; division
Human Hazards: Spiny
Major Pest Problems: None
Major Disease or Physiological Problems: None
Cultivars: A dwarf variety *gonsalezii* has been described

Morphology (Identifying Characteristics)

Habit: Clustering tightly; canopy of about 20 leaves per trunk
Trunk or Stem characteristics: Slender, covered with burlap-like matting and rings of sharp, spiny fibers
Leaf Type: Palmate, induplicate, slightly folded; divided to 1/2-2/3 into 30-40 segments that droop and are slightly split at tips; 3-pointed hastula
Foliage Color: Bright green above, silver below
Leaf Size: 2-3' wide; segments 2' long, 1-2" wide
Petiole: 4' long, very thin, unarmed
Crownshaft: None
Inflorescence: 1.5' long, twice-branched
Gender: Bisexual flowers
Flower color: White
Fruit Size: 1" diameter
Fruit Color: White
Irritant: No

Comments: This unusual fan palm is closely related to *Coccothrinax* and *Thrinax* and has been known to hybridize with species of the former genus. The tightly clustering stems eventually produce a beautiful specimen plant, on no small account due to the intricate weaving of leaf stem base fibers that envelop the trunk. These should be admired at a comfortable distance, however, since the end of the fibers project outward and upward as sharp spines. The evocative name of the species is derived from the alleged use of these spines as voodoo doll needles. Zombie palm prefers a very well-drained soil and a situation in full sun.

SECTION II

What Is A Palm?

Palms, though capable of reaching tree-like dimensions, differ from typical broad-leaved trees in profound ways that affect aspects of their cultivation. Palms belong to the division of the flowering plants known as the **monocots**. This group includes the lilies, grasses, irises, orchids and bromeliads. Most monocot families consist of primarily herbaceous plants, that is, low-growing, soft-tissued plants. Very few other species of monocots attain the size of many palms. This is largely due to certain constraints placed on the development of the stems of monocots which in turn distinguish them from the second division of flowering plants, called dicots. All of our favorite flowering trees and shrubs, and most of our shade trees, are dicots. Oaks, maples, azaleas, roses and most garden annuals are dicots.

Dicots have a developmental feature that virtually all monocots lack. Within the stems of woody dicots, the water and food conducting tissue occurs in complete, concentric rings. In monocots, these same **vascular tissues** occur in bundles scattered throughout the internal tissue of the stem, rather than in complete rings. In dicots, a specialized layer of cells called the **vascular cambium** is formed between the water conducting rings (**xylem**) and the food conducting rings (**phloem**). The vascular cambium produces new rings of xylem toward the inside of the stem, and new rings of phloem toward the outside. For the vast majority of monocots, including all palms, no vascular cambium exists.

What is the consequence of having or not having a vascular cambium? Woody dicots, blessed by nature with a vascular cambium, are capable of what plant scientists call **secondary growth.** This means that a dicot tree stem is always producing new vascular tissue and increasing in diameter as it ages. The vascular cambium also allows a dicot tree to repair injuries to its stem fairly efficiently, and horticulturists to successfully graft stems or buds of one species or variety onto the stem of another closely related species. This ability to produce secondary growth is evident in the pattern of growth rings that can be seen in a cross-section of a woody dicot stem.

Unlike an oak tree or an apple tree, palms are essentially incapable of secondary growth and do not produce annual growth rings. Once a palm stem achieves its maximum girth at a given point on the stem, it is largely incapable of increasing its stem diameter. Furthermore, the bundles of conducting tissue within the palm stem must last the entire life of the palm. Once a palm stem achieves its maximum diameter, not one single additional vascular bundle will be added to the internal tissue of the stem! Palms are also not able to repair their vascular bundles if damage is received to the stem. And, not surprisingly, it is impossible to graft one part of a palm to another. Most importantly of all, the future of a palm stem rides upon the continued health of a single actively growing bud or "palm heart" with little or no ability to regenerate itself. Very few palms have the ability to branch on their aerial stems. Thus, if the palm heart is killed, the entire palm (if solitary) or the palm stem (if clustering) is doomed to eventual death.

With this in mind, it becomes all the more remarkable that palms have been able to reach such scales of height as they are indeed capable. P. B. Tomlinson of Harvard University, who has studied the structural biology of palms in detail, likens their stems (fibrous vascular bundles scattered in pithy stem tissue) to steel-reinforced concrete, a telling analogy indeed!

How Palms Grow

Unlike broad-leaved trees, palms complete their thickening growth or increase in diameter before elongating. This is most evident in those palms that do not develop a conspicuous aerial trunk for a number of years (*Sabal* spp., for example), but is true for all palm species. During this "establishment phase," as Tomlinson has called it, the palm is particularly sensitive to growth checks or less than optimal conditions.

Root system. Typical of all monocots, the functioning root system of a palm develops from the stem. Very shortly after seed germination, the seedling root of a palm ceases to function and is replaced by roots produced from a specialized area of the stem called the **root initiation zone.** It is during the establishment phase of its growth that a young palm fully develops this initiation zone at the base of the stem. Such roots, originating from the stem, are called **adventitious,** in contrast to the underground root systems of dicots which develop sequentially from a perennial seedling root. Again, unlike dicots, palm roots emerge from the stem at maximum thickness; they are incapable of secondary growth. They can branch, however, to three levels. The third rank of root branches are the thinnest and function primarily in absorption of water and nutrients. Palm roots do not produce root hairs. Palm roots are capable of significant lateral growth; roots of some palms have been measured well over a hundred feet from the parent trunk. On some palms the root initiation zone extends for some distance above ground level on the trunk. Most extreme in this regard are the "stilt-root" palms of tropical rain forests that produce long, thick support roots from as high as 6-10 feet above the trunk base. Extensions of the root initiation zone can also be seen on those date palm species that produce a mass of aerial roots stubs at the trunk base. A few palms (*Chamaedorea* spp.) form aerial roots all along their stems.

Palm stems. The stems or trunks of palms are as diverse as the palms themselves, varying in thickness, shape, surface features and habit. Though none are treated in this book, a sizable group of palms even grow as high climbing vines into the canopies of rain forest trees. Many palm stems remain covered with the remains of old leaf bases for many years (Fig. 1); others shed their dead leaves very readily. For the first years of a palm's life, the stem consists of little more than overlapping leaf bases shielding the all important bud or palm heart. Some palm trunks swell noticeably at the base as they develop with age; others develop conspicuous bulges further up on the stem. Most tall growing palms eventually produce a clear trunk, usually gray or brown, sometimes green (Fig. 2). The trunks of some palms are conspicuously spiny; these spines are often the remains of fibers that occurred within the tissue of the leaf bases. The scars left behind by fallen leaves frequently create a distinctive pattern on the trunk. These may appears as rings, or, if the leaves incompletely sheath the trunk, variously shaped scars. The point on the stem at which a leaf scar occurs (or where a leaf is still attached) is called a **node**. Very few palms are capable of branching on their aerial stems in the normal course of their growth; occasionally an aberrant individual of an otherwise non-branching species will produce a branched head.

Palm leaves. The leaves of palms are the largest such organs in the plant kingdom. All palm leaves consist of three main parts (Fig. 3a): the **blade,** the **petiole** or leaf stem, and the **leaf base.** The leaf base is basically that part of the petiole that sheathes the stem. On many palms, the base remains attached to the trunk for some time after the blade and the petiole drop off. In some cases, the pattern of leaf base stubs is a distinctive feature of the palm's appearance. The tubular leaf bases of some feather-leafed palms sheath each other so tightly around the stem that they form a conspicuous neck-like structure called a **crownshaft** (Fig. 2). Often waxy and smooth, and sometimes attractively colored, the crownshaft is usually a structure of singular beauty. The leaf stem or petiole can be short or long; in a few species it is apparently obsolete. The petiole of a number of palm species is toothed along the margins, ferociously so in some.

Palm leaf blades basically fall into three main classes, palmate or costapalmate (the fan palms), pinnate or bipinnate leaves (the feather

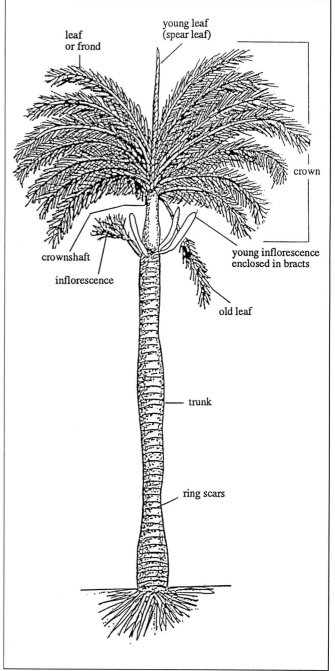

Figure 2. Structures of a palm.

Figure 1. Trunk of paurotis palm (*Acoelorraphe wrightii*).

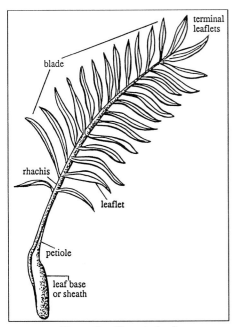

Figure 3a. Pinnate leaf.

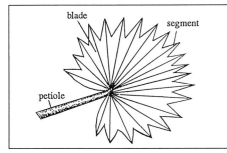

Figure 4a. Palmate leaf.

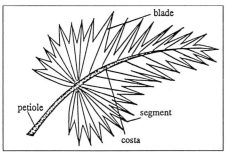

Figure 4b. Costapalmate leaf.

palms), or entire leaves. The fan palms are classified as either **palmate** (Fig. 4a) or **costapalmate** (Fig. 4b). Fan palm leaves are circular or shaped like an out-stretched hand. They are divided shallowly or deeply into a variable number of **segments** which are often split at the tips themselves. Palmate and costapalmate leaves are similar in appearance except for the extension of the leaf stem (petiole) into the blade of the costapalmate leaf. This extension is sometimes referred to as the **costa**. Costapalmate leaves are often twisted or folded sharply along or at the tip of the costa. Many fan palms have an additional feature called the **hastula** (Fig. 5) that is sometimes useful in identifying the species. The hastula is a small, thin, more-or-less rounded protuberance of tissue located at the point where the petiole meets the blade. Hastulas are most frequently located on the upper surface of the leaf; a few fan palms have them on both surfaces. It is blunt or pointed at the tip, and its function is unknown.

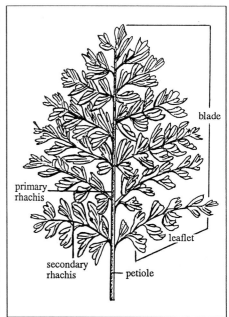

Figure 3b. Bipinnate.

Feather palm leaves consist of a network of individual leaflets arrayed along an extension of the leaf stem called the **rachis. Pinnately compound** (Fig. 3a) palm leaves are feather leaves that are only once-compound; that is, there is only a single series of leaflets. The leaflets may be numerous or few, narrow or broad, pointed at the tip or blunt and toothed. They can be regularly arranged along the rachis or attached in groups of several. **Bipinnately compound** (Fig. 3b) palm leaves are twice-compound; that is, the primary leaflets themselves consist of a system of smaller secondary leaflets. Bipinnately compound leaves are very rare in the palm family, occurring in only a single tribe (Caryoteae) of the subfamily Arecoideae. Entire-leafed palms have neither segments nor leaflets. Instead, the leaf consists of an unsplit (or at most two-lobed) blade, longer than it is wide. Of the palms treated in this book, only one species, *Chamaedorea metallica*, has an entire leaf. Interestingly, the first leaves of many palm seedlings are entire, regardless of what type of mature leaf occurs on the palm.

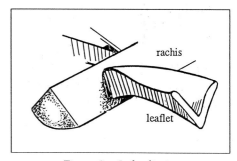

Figure 6a. Induplicate.

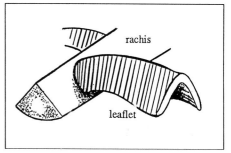

Figure 6b. Reduplicate.

Figure 5. Hastula on upper surface of fan palm leaf.

Induplicate vs. Reduplicate Leaves. An important feature of palm leaves that has significance in the taxonomy and identification of the major groups within the family is the way in which the leaf segments (fan palms) or leaflets (feather palms) are folded around the main vein or midrib. Palms in which the leaflets or segments are folded upward, forming a "V", are called **induplicate** (Fig. 6a). Palms in which the leaflets or segments are folded downward, forming an inverted "V", are termed **reduplicate** (Fig. 6b). Most of the fan palms have induplicate leaves, while the majority of the feather palms have reduplicate leaves. The best place to look to determine which type of folding characterizes a particular species is right at the point where the leaflet attaches to the rachis (feather palms) or, on fan palms, the point where the segments first split from the rest of the leaf.

Figure 7. Flowers of Senegal date palm (*Phoenix reclinata*).

Figure 8. Flowers of King Alexander palm (*Archontophoenix alexandrae*).

Figure 9. Male flowers of lady palm (*Rhapis excelsa*).

Palm flowers. The individual flowers of a palm are generally quite small and inconspicuous, but are usually borne in such numbers on the flower stalk or **inflorescence** (Fig. 2) that they collectively are showy (Figs. 7-10). The inflorescences of palms are frequently quite long and much-branched, but on some species they are short and spike-like (unbranched). On palms with crownshafts, the flower stalks are usually produced from the trunk below the crownshaft, and thus below all the leaves as well. On palms without crownshafts, the inflorescences emerge from among the leaves. On a few palms whose stems flower once (*Corypha* spp. and *Nannorrhops ritchiana*), the flower stalks appear to originate at the tips of the stems. Some palm flower stalks are backed by a large, boat-like **bract** or **spathe** that may persist even in fruit.

Figure 10. Flowers of clustering fishtail palm (*Caryota mitis*).

The parts of the simplest palm flowers occur in three's or multiples thereof; however; there is an enormous amount of variation in flower structure throughout the family. Likewise, palms vary greatly in the gender allocation of their flowers. Some have bisexual flowers with both functional male and female reproductive organs. Many palms have separate male and female flowers on the same plant, usually on the same inflorescence. Other palm species produce separate male and female plants altogether, with flowers of only one sex occurring on any one particular plant. All date palms (*Phoenix* spp.) fit in this third category. The small size and fairly bland coloration of most palm flowers first led botanists to conclude that most palms were pollinated by wind. It is now known that, in fact, most palms are insect pollinated.

Figure 11. Fruits of cabbage palm (*Sabal palmetto*).

Palm fruits and seeds. In contrast to the often diminutive flowers, the fruits (and seed as well) of many palm species are fairly large and conspicuous (Figs. 11-14). In fact, the largest seed of any plant known on the face of the earth belongs to a palm, the double coconut (*Lodoicea maldavica*). The majority of palm fruits are classified as drupes. A **drupe** is defined as a fleshy, one-seeded fruit that does not open or split at maturity. Some palm fruits qualify as berries or even nuts (the coconut, for example). A number of palm fruits contain more than one seed, but the majority carry only one seed within. The fruits of most palms have a fleshy or fibrous outer wall that is frequently attractively colored. For more than a few species, the display afforded by the ripe fruits is much more conspicuous than that of the flowers! The seed within a palm fruit is protected by a bony or fibrous coat. The seed coat of some species bears interesting patterns of ornamentation or sculpturing on its surface. Most of the volume of the seed is taken up by the nutritive tissue called endosperm that feeds the developing seedling. The actual embryo of a palm is quite small, and is located in a small chamber at one end of the seed.

Figure 12. Fruits of Christmas palm (*Veitchia merrillii*).

Figure 13. Fruits of queen palm (*Syagrus romanzoffiana*).

Classification Of The Palm Family

The palm family, consisting of 2300-2700 species, is known to botanists as the **Palmae** or the **Arecaceae**. That branch of botany devoted to formulating the classification of plants is called taxonomy. Relative to many other large and economically important plant families, the Arecaceae has not been well studied taxonomically, largely due to the difficulty in preparing dried field specimens of palms, and the fact that well over 90% of the palm family's diversity is found in the tropics. In 1987, a landmark occurred in the taxonomic history of the palm family with the publication of *Genera Palmarum* by Drs. Natalie Uhl of Cornell University's Bailey Hortorium and John Dransfield of the Royal Botanic Gardens at Kew. Inspired by years of work at the Bailey Hortorium by the late Harold Moore, *Genera Palmarum* presented the first complete, modern system of classification for the palm family through the rank of genus (a group of related species believed to be of common ancestry and defined by certain important shared characteristics that sets them apart from other species groups).

Uhl and Dransfield recognized 200 genera (the plural for genus) in the palm family. These genera are organized into six **subfamilies** defined by certain important characteristics shared by all the component genera. The subfamilies in turn are subdivided into **tribes.** These subfamilies and tribes are listed below. Those containing genera treated in this book are in boldface, and the particular genera treated are listed in parentheses.

Figure 14. Fruits of King Alexander palm
(*Archontophoenix alexandrae*).

Family **ARECACEAE** or **PALMAE**

Subfamily **Arecoideae**
Tribe **Areceae:** (*Archontophoenix, Areca, Carpentaria, Chrysalidocarpus, Cyrtostachys, Dictyosperma, Euterpe, Neodypsis, Pinanga, Ptychosperma, Roystonea, Veitchia, Wodyetia*)
Tribe **Caryoteae:** (*Arenga, Caryota*)
Tribe **Cocoeae:** (*Acrocomia, Allagoptera, Bactris, Butia, Cocos, Elaeis, Heterospathe, Howea, Jubaea, Syagrus*)
Tribe Geonomeae
Tribe Iriarteae
Tribe Podococceae

Subfamily Calamoideae
Tribe Calameae
Tribe Lepidocaryeae

Subfamily **Ceroxyloideae**
Tribe **Cyclospatheae:** (*Pseudophoenix*)
Tribe **Ceroxyleae:**   (*Ravenea*)
Tribe **Hyophorbeae:** (*Chamaedorea, Gaussia, Hyophorbe*)

Subfamily **Coryphoideae**
Tribe **Borasseae:** (*Bismarckia, Borassus, Hyphaene, Latania*)
Tribe **Corypheae:** (*Acoelorrhaphe, Brahea, Chamaerops, Coccothrinax, Copernicia, Corypha, Licuala, Livistona, Nannorrhops, Pritchardia, Rhapidophyllum, Rhapis, Sabal, Serenoa, Thrinax, Trachycarpus, Trithrinax, Washingtonia, Zombia*)
Tribe **Phoeniceae:** (*Phoenix*)

Subfamily Nypoideae

Subfamily Phytelephantoideae

Conservation Of Palms

No horticulturist working in the tropics or subtropics can afford to be indifferent to the loss of biodiversity that is currently taking place throughout the world's tropics, fueled in part by the desire of tropical, Third World countries to achieve the status of First World economies and deal with explosive population growth, but in equal measure caused by the developed nations' insatiable appetite for world resources to support affluent and frequently wasteful lifestyles. Palms are first and foremost a tropical plant family, and numerous species are known only from single populations or inhabit restricted ranges of distribution. In the past, palms were sometimes spared from destruction because the fibrous trunks would very quickly dull the blades of axes, but in these days of chainsaws and wholesale forest burning, rain forest palms are as easily reduced to ash and charred stumps as any other tree.

While horticulture can help in the preservation of many rare palms that might otherwise disappear off the face of the earth, conservation of palms in their intact habitats also preserves their unique relationships to their natural environment, from the insects that pollinate their flowers, to the animals that eat their fruit. A number of palm species are now represented in cultivation by more individuals than ever existed in the wild. Nonetheless, over-zealous collection of seeds or plants from the wild can also place pressure on rare palms. Within the world of palm horticulture, horror stories circulate about rare palms being cut down in order that their seed crop could be collected and sold. Palm horticulturists need to become more sensitive to the source of the palms in commerce. Do not purchase rare palms that have been collected from the wild, unless you know for a fact that their habitat was slated for destruction or development.

The International Palm Society

The International Palm Society is a not-for-profit organization devoted to the support of palm research, education, conservation, and cultivation. The Society has a number of local chapters in the United States and abroad, publishes a high quality and informative quarterly journal called *Principes*, manages a seed fund for members from which seed of many rare palms can be purchased for nominal cost, and holds a biennial meeting in various locations around the world that draws members internationally. For membership information write to: International Palm Society, P. 0. Box 1897, Lawrence KS 66044, USA.

References

Tomlinson, P. B. 1990. *The Structural Biology of Palms.* Clarendon Press, Oxford
Uhl, N. W. and J. Dransfield. 1987. *Genera Palmarum.* International Palm Society, Allen Press, Lawrence, KS.

Fertilizing Palms

Landscape Palm Fertilization Programs

The frequency with which landscape palms need to be fertilized depends greatly on the type of soil in which they are planted and the amount of rainfall (or irrigation) that they will receive. In Florida, for example, poor, shallow soils coupled with heavy rainfall during the growing season results in a very low natural reservoir of essential plant nutrients. Thus mature palms in the Florida landscape should optimally receive a complete granular fertilizer formulated for palms ("palm special") three-four times per year at a rate of 5-8 lbs each application. "Palm special" fertilizers contain additional magnesium and a complete micronutrient ("trace mineral") amendment. Dropping below a minimum of two applications, even for the most budget conscious maintenance schedules, is not recommended. In California, rainfall is lower, soils are generally of much higher quality, and the nutrient holding capacity of these soils should allow less frequent application of fertilizer. Elsewhere, palms planted on loamy, organic, or clay based soils may also get by with less fertilizer.

Dry, granular fertilizers should be broadcast or banded under the canopy of the palm, but should not be placed up against the trunk where newly emerging roots may be injured. If granular fertilizers will be used in conjunction with drip irrigation systems, the fertilizer should be banded directly below the drip emitters. Nitrogen and potassium rates in the formulation should be equivalent, and at least some of both elements should be available in slow release form. The blend should also contain magnesium at about 1/3 the rate of the nitrogen and potassium.

For palms under eight feet tall, 2-5 lbs of fertilizer per feeding should be adequate. Newly planted palms can receive even less (1/2 to 2 lbs, depending on size). A reasonable formula to use is 1/2 lb of fertilizer per 2 feet of overall height, up to about 15 lbs for a mature specimen (greater than 30' in height).

Where rapid leaching of nutrients is not a problem, root zone drenches with or shallow injection of soluble fertilizer blends can also be used. On very sandy soils, especially in high rainfall areas, much of the nutrients in soluble, liquid fertilizers will be removed from the root zone before they can be absorbed by the palm's roots.

Foliar feeds

Foliar fertilization is an inefficient method for providing macronutrient elements such as nitrogen, phosphorus, potassium, and magnesium due to the large amounts required by the palm, but is very useful for supplying micronutrients such as manganese and iron to the plants when soil conditions prevent adequate uptake of these elements by the roots. Foliar fertilization is best used as a supplement for a normal soil fertilization program, particularly for micronutrients.

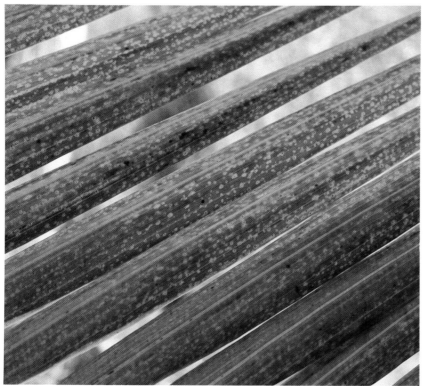

Figure 15. Early "flecking" stage of potassium deficiency.

Nutritional Disorders In The Landscape

Palms suffer quickly and conspicuously from improper mineral nutrition, whether due to insufficient or incorrect fertilization. They also may exhibit certain nutritional disorders in unique ways compared to other ornamental plants. Some nutritional problems in palms are difficult to diagnose accurately because symptoms of several different mineral deficiencies may overlap. The following are the most common nutritional deficiencies likely to be encountered in the landscape.

Nitrogen (N)

An overall light green color and decreased vigor of the palm are indicative of N deficiency. It is usually only seen in the landscape on palms planted in infertile soils without supplementary fertilization. Application of any fertilizer containing nitrogen will quickly improve the color of the foliage.

Figure 16. Potassium deficiency on thatch palm (*Thrinax* sp.).

Potassium (K)

This deficiency is very common in Florida where soils are naturally deficient in potassium and are quickly leached of this very soluble mineral element. In California, it is not a conspicuous problem. Symptoms vary among palm species, but always occur first on oldest leaves and affects progressively newer leaves as the deficiency becomes more severe. On many palms, the early symptoms are translucent yellow or orange flecks on the leaflets or segments (Fig. 15), with or without necrotic spots. Areas of necrosis often

Figure 17. Later stages of potassium deficiency on coconut (*Cocos nucifera*).

can be seen along the margins. On some species, marginal necrosis is the typical first sign of deficiency (Fig. 16). As the symptoms progress, the entire leaf appears burnt and withered (Fig. 17). In date palms (*Phoenix* spp.) symptoms are slightly different in that older leaves show an orange-brown or dull yellow discoloration near the tip (Fig. 18), in contrast to the bright yellow of magnesium deficiency (Fig. 19). The leaflet tips, rather than the margins, become necrotic as the deficiency progresses. When all available potassium has been shunted from the older leaves to the new growth, the palm declines. "Pencil-pointing" (an abrupt reduction in trunk diameter) and the emergence of small, frizzled or chlorotic new leaves indicate that without immediate treatment, the palm will probably die. Potassium deficiency affects most palms, but in Florida the most susceptible species are royal, queen, coconut, areca, and spindle palms. Treatment requires soil applications of potassium sulfate at rates of 3-8 lbs. per tree 4 times per year plus 1/3 to 1/2 as much magnesium sulfate to prevent a potassium-magnesium imbalance (and resulting magnesium deficiency) from occurring. Symptomatic leaves on K-deficient palms will never recover and must be replaced by new, healthy leaves. In severely deficient palms, this means replacing the entire canopy which may take 2 years or longer. Foliar sprays with K fertilizers are ineffective in correcting the problem since the amount of K supplied by a foliar spray is insignificant compared to the amount needed to correct the problem.

Figure 18. Early potassium deficiency on pygmy date palm (*Phoenix roebelenii*).

Magnesium (Mg)

Magnesium deficiency is very common in Florida, and anywhere else where palms are planted on poor, infertile soils. Date palms (*Phoenix* spp.) are particularly susceptible. Visible symptoms begin on the oldest leaves and progress upward to the younger foliage, typically a broad light yellow band along the margin of the older leaves with the center of the leaf remaining green (Figs. 19 and 20). In severe cases, leaflet tips may become necrotic, but Mg deficiency is rarely if ever fatal to palms. Magnesium defi-

Figure 19. Magnesium deficiency on date palm (*Phoenix dactylifera*).

ciency is best treated preventatively since treatment of deficient palms takes considerable time. As with K deficiency, symptomatic leaves will never recover and must be replaced by new healthy leaves. Applications of magnesium sulfate (epsom salts) at rates of 2-4 lbs per tree 4 times per year should correct the problem.

Manganese (Mn)

Manganese deficiency or "frizzletop" is a common problem in palms growing in alkaline soils, because this element is relatively insoluble at high pH. Symptoms occur only on new leaves which emerge chlorotic, weak, reduced in size, and with extensive necrotic streaking in the leaves. As the deficiency progresses, succeeding leaves will emerge completely withered, frizzled, or scorched in appearance and greatly reduced in size (Fig. 21). Later, only necrotic petiole stubs will emerge and death of the bud quickly follows.

In some palms such as coconut, which are not normally affected by the problem, cold soil temperatures during the winter and spring months reduce root activity and thus the uptake of micronutrients (especially Mn). Coconut palms severely deficient in Mn during the winter and spring will usually grow out of the problem without special

Figure 20. Magnesium deficiency on date palm (*Phoenix dactylifera*).

treatment once soil temperatures warm up in late spring. Other palms such as queen, royal, paurotis, and pygmy date palms, are highly susceptible to Mn deficiency and must be treated with soil or foliar applications of manganese sulfate or they will likely die.

Iron (Fe)

Iron deficiency is relatively uncommon in landscape palms and is not usually caused by a lack of Fe in the soil, or even by high soil pH, as in many other plants. Iron deficiency usually appears on palms growing in poorly aerated soils or those that have been planted too deeply. Waterlogged soils and deep planting effectively suffocate the roots. Symptoms appear first on the new leaves and in most palms consists of uniformly chlorotic new leaves (Fig. 22), with green coloration entirely restricted to the veins of the new leaves. As the deficiency progresses, new leaves will show extensive dead tissue at the tips (necrosis) and reduced leaf

Figure 21. "Frizzletop" caused by manganese deficiency on coconut (*Cocos nucifera*).

size. Iron deficiency symptoms can sometimes be temporarily alleviated by regular foliar applications of iron sulfate or chelates, but long term correction will only occur when the poor soil aeration or improper planting depth that caused the deficiency is corrected. It is also important to remember that any injury to the root system can cause nutritional deficiencies to appear.

Diagnosis of nutrient deficiencies by visual symptoms alone can be difficult, since some of the symptoms overlap considerably in some species. For instance, Mn and late-stage K deficiencies are easily confused on queen and royal palms. Potassium and Mg deficiencies are very similar in pygmy date palms and K and Fe deficiencies can be very similar in royal palms. If complex symptoms defy a simple diagnosis, it is wise to have a diagnostic laboratory perform a leaf nutrient analysis before undertaking any corrective action.

Figure 22. Iron deficiency on lady palm (*Rhapis excelsa*).

References

Broschat, T. K. and A. W. Meerow. 1990. *Palm Nutrition Guide*. University of Florida Extension Circular SS-ORH-02.

Transplanting And Landscape Care Of Palms

Young palms (that is, without visible trunk development) should only be transplanted from containers. Palms are not very tolerant of the extreme root disturbance that accompanies digging from a field nursery or previous landscape site until visible trunk development has taken place. This is most critical for species that characteristically complete a great deal of stem development deeply below ground (for example, *Bismarckia noblilis, Latania* spp., *Sabal* spp.). Even if the palms are not killed by premature transplanting, growth setbacks and possibly less than optimum caliper development may occur.

Palms establish most quickly if transplanted during the spring and early summer when soils temperatures are on the increase. Many tropical palms exhibit reduced root function at soil temperatures below 65° F, thus winter planting should be avoided if possible when tropical species are being used in slightly more temperate zones. In the tropics, time of year is not as critical from the perspective of temperature, though planting should coincide with the rainy season in order to reduce the need for supplementary irrigation during the first critical months of establishment.

Figure 23. Typical manually dug root ball for a palm less than 15' in height.

Root Ball Size

From the list of palms whose root regeneration patterns have been studied (Table 1, page 122) it appears that the most common response is (1) some degree of branching of cut roots, the percentage increasing with the length of the stub (up to a point) accompanied by (2) some variable degree of new root initiation from the trunk base. In general, for single-stemmed palms less than 15 feet in height, a root ball of shovel's width radius from the trunk is a common industry average for size and should provide for adequate root survival in those species exhibiting that response (Fig. 23). For clustering or larger solitary specimens, an incrementally larger root ball may be advisable to insure successful establishment under site conditions that may be less than ideal. An obvious concern for the field grower is to minimize loss of soil from the field. A one foot minimum radius (from the trunk) is recommended for these palms. While a larger root ball may well increase transplant success, the additional weight and costs involved in transportation may not justify the slight gains in post transplant survival.

Queen palms will likely survive if dug with a minimum root ball of 6" radius from the trunk, but a larger root ball will increase root survival at the landscape site. Root branching in coconut palms (*Cocos nucifera*) does not appear to be dependent on the size of the root ball. In sabal palms (*Sabal palmetto*), virtually all of which are dug from native stands rather than nursery grown, negligible root branching occurs, and new roots must be initiated from the trunk. For these two species, smaller root balls are acceptable.

Root Pruning

Root pruning has generally not been considered necessary for palms, with the exception of Bismarck palm (*Bismarckia nobilis*) and a few others. However, if the species is a particularly high value palm for which replacement costs would be expensive, the extra labor may well be cost effective. For palms that must regenerate new roots from the trunk, root-pruning 2-3 months before digging should provide adequate time for new root growth within the ball.

When moving palms out of the field, they should be well supported to prevent injury to the tender heart. Some palms (for example, King Alexander, *Archontophoenix alexandrae*) are much more sensitive to heart injury due to rough handling than others, and require extra care in transport. For certain species with slender trunks (for example, Senegal date, *Phoenix reclinata*; paurotis palm, *Acoelorrhaphe wrightii*), a supporting splint should be tied to each trunk and should extend into the foliage to protect the bud. Palms with very heavy crowns (for example, Canary Island date palm, *Phoenix canariensis*) should be braced similarly to prevent the weight of the crown from snapping the bud. Stems of clustering palms should also be tied together for additional support. A tree crane is usually required to lift large palms out of the field, and the trunk should be protected with burlap or other material wherever ropes, cables, chains or straps will be attached (Fig. 24)

Leaf Removal

The greatest loss of water in newly dug palms occurs from transpiration through the leaves. To minimize this, one half or more of the leaves should be removed at the time of digging. The remaining leaves should be tied together in a bundle around the bud with a biodegradable twine. The best method of insuring survival after transplanting into the landscape may be to remove ALL leaves on species like sabal palms that must regenerate all new roots from the trunk. Sabal palms have repeatedly exhibited higher establishment success rates when all leaves are removed when they are dug. Complete leaf removal may also be advisable during installation of any species where normal post-transplant irrigation is impossible. However, many buyers will object to this practice for aesthetic reasons. Where practical, misting or irrigation of the foliage may reduce water loss during the transplant process, though there is an accompanying risk of increasing disease problems in the canopy.

Figure 24. Tree crane used to lift a specimen size palm.

Site Preparation

It is always best to install newly dug specimen palms immediately to minimize stress and possible loss of the palm. If delivered palms cannot be planted immediately upon arrival at the installation site, the palms should be placed out of direct sun and the trunk, root ball and canopy kept moist. Temporarily "heeling in" the root balls under a layer of mulch is advisable, especially if other no means of keeping the roots from drying out is available.

Installation site conditions also contribute to the establishment success of transplanted palms. A well drained location is essential; standing water should not appear at the bottom of the planting hole. If drainage is a problem at the site, a berm should be constructed to raise the root ball above the level of water. Though some palm species may adjust to less than optimal drainage after establishment, standing water around a newly dug root ball will have adverse effects on root regeneration.

The planting hole should be wide enough to easily accept the root ball and provide at least several inches of new growth from the ball. It need only be deep enough to situate the palm at the same depth at which it previously grew. The amending of backfill soil from the planting hole is not recommended, unless the surrounding site soil has also been amended. If the backfill soil differs greatly in structure and texture from the surrounding site soil, new roots will have a tendency to remain within the backfill. If amending the backfill soil is demanded, the volume of amendment should not exceed 25% of the soil removed from the hole.

Planting and Support

Planting Depth

In general, palms should not be transplanted any deeper than they were originally grown. The root initiation zone of most palms (located at the base of the trunk) is sensitive in this regard, and planting too deeply can cause root suffocation, nutritional deficiencies, root rot disease and perhaps ultimately the loss of the palm. Unfortunately, it is still a common practice for installers to situate specimen-sized palms at various depths in order to create a planting of uniform height. The decline of deeply planted palms may take several years to become apparent, especially on very well-drained soils, but it can only be reversed by removing the backfill from the suffocated root initiation zone or replanting the palm.

All air pockets should be tamped out of the backfill as the planting hole is filled. A berm should be mounded up at the periphery of the root ball to retain water during irrigation. The initial irrigation should be deep and thorough. Filling the planting hole with water up to the berm will be necessary 2-3 times to fully wet and settle the soil.

Support

Larger palms will require some form of bracing to maintain stability during the first 6-8 months after installation. The proper method of support is illustrated in Figure 25. Short lengths of 2" x 4" lumber should be banded or strapped to the trunk (a foundation of burlap or asphalt paper can be placed around the trunk under these), and support braces (also 2" x 4", or 4" x 4" on very large specimens) are then nailed into them. Under no circumstances should nails be driven directly into a palm trunk. Such damage is permanent, and provides entryway for pathogens and possibly insect pests as well.

Figure 25. The proper method of supporting a newly installed large palm specimen.

Establishment Care

The root ball and surrounding backfill should remain evenly moist, but never saturated during the first 4-6 months after installation. Supplementary irrigation is necessary unless adequate rainfall is received during this time period. Newly transplanted specimen-sized palms should not be expected to produce a great deal of new top growth during the first year after transplanting; much of the palm's energy reserves will (and should) be channeled into root growth. Drenching the root zone 2-4 times during the first few months with a fungicide labelled for landscape use on soil borne root fungal pathogens is recommended for high value palms. A light surface application of a partially slow-release "palm special" granular fertilizer can be banded at the margins of the root ball 3-4 months after transplanting. A foliar spray of soluble micronutrients may be beneficial during this period, since root absorption activity is limited. Macronutrients (nitrogen, phosphorous, potassium, magnesium) cannot be supplied through the leaves in sufficient quantity to feed the palm, and should generally not be applied as a foliar feed. When the appearance of new leaves indicates that establishment has been successful, a regular fertilization program can begin.

Table 1. Root system responses of selected palm species to digging after approximately 5 months[1].		
Species	Branching	New root initiation
Cocos nucifera (Coconut)	50% cut roots branch regardless of stub length	Low[2] (20 or less)
Phoenix reclinata (Senegal date)	33% cut roots branch if stubs are at least 2' long	Moderate (about 60)
Roystonea regia (Cuban royal)	24% cut roots branch if stubs are 1-2' long; 36% if 2-3' long	High (about 100)
Sabal palmetto (Cabbage palm)	Negligible	Very high (about 200)
Syagrus romanzoffiana[3] (Queen palm)	41% cut roots branch if stubs are 6"-1' long	Low (13)
Washingtonia robusta (Mexican fan)	31% cut roots branch if stubs are 1-2' long; 58% if stubs are 2-3' long	Very high (about 150)

[1] All data from Broschat and Donselman 1984a and b, 1990 (see References).
[2] May increase with age
[3] Redug after 18 weeks of regrowth

Landscape Use and Care of Palms

A well established palm in the landscape is largely a low maintenance item as long as a regular program of fertilization and irrigation suitable to the conditions of the landscape site and the needs of the particular species is received. Overwatering can be detrimental to palms that are adapted for dry conditions, and can lead to various disease problems (see Diseases of Landscape Palms, page 128), while failure to provide adequate water to a wet rain forest dwelling palm can result in poor growth and even loss of the plant.

Palms are best planted in a situation where turf grass can be kept away from the trunk. Even a small mulched circle around the base of a palm is better than allowing turf to grow right up to the trunk base. The main reason for this is the prevention of trunk injuries from weed eaters, mowers and other lawn care equipment. Such wounds are permanent, and allow the entrance of disease organisms such as the *Ganoderma* fungus, and possibly some insect pests as well. Palms from arid regions are often not compatible with turf oriented irrigation schedules, and such species are best not planted as lawn specimens if irrigation will be frequent and shallow. Turf will also compete for water and nutrients with palms planted within the lawn, and growth may not be optimum when compared to the same palm planted in a large, mulched landscape bed.

Within a landscape bed, consideration must be given to the compatibility of the palms to be used with the other plants that will be included. Will the massing of ground covers or annual flowers near the base of the palm create difficulty in properly fertilizing the palm? Will the water needs of the shrubs, ground covers or flowers in the bed prove detrimental to the palm? The high cost of replacing or moving specimen palms necessitates that one ask these questions before installation.

Where to Use Palms in the Landscape

Palm can be used for a variety of purposes in the landscape. While few palms can really provide the same measure of shade relative to a broad-leaved tree, tall growing cluster palms or group plantings of solitary palms can function as shade trees for a small home or for a quiet nook in the backyard. Tall growing palms provide a strong vertical accent in the landscape, and can overpower a small building. For example, royal palms (*Roystonea* spp.) planted near a small home only serve to make the house appear smaller.

Tall, solitary palms make effective border or boundary plantings for lining a long driveway or boulevard, while most tall clustering palms are effective as single accent specimens. The bold aspect of many palms draws attention to the area of the landscape that they inhabit.

Palms combine as well with each other as they do with other types of landscape plants. A well-designed bed of various palm species can be the focal point of a subtropical landscape. Growth rates, habit, and eventual size must be considered carefully when combining species to avoid a helter skelter mix that fails aesthetically. Small groves of the same species can also create an attractive landscape accent. King Alexander (*Archontophoenix alexandrae*), various *Veitchia* species and many other slender or moderate trunked species can be grouped successfully in the landscape. Densely clustering species such as the lady palms (*Rhapis* spp.), some *Chamaedorea* species, and areca (*Chrysalidocarpus lutescens*) can be used to create a screen. Avoid planting tall growing palms directly under roof overhangs and eaves. A misplaced palm is one that will one day have to be removed.

Pruning Palms

Palms do not require pruning as we associate the term with branching, broad-leaved trees. The only trimming any palm needs is the removal of dead or badly damaged or diseased leaves. There is an unfortunate tendency for landscape maintenance workers to overtrim palms, removing perfectly good, green, functional leaves at the same time as dead or dying fronds are trimmed. The logic behind this practice, no doubt, is an attempt to lengthen the interval before trimming is once again necessary. The removal of healthy leaves is a disservice to the palm, especially those species whose canopy consists of no more than 8-12 leaves. Overtrimming reduces the food manufacturing efficiency of the living palm and can result in sub-optimum caliper development at the point in the crown where diameter increase is currently taking place. There is also some evidence that overtrimming makes the palm more susceptible to cold damage.

References

Broschat, T. K. 1991. "Effects of leaf removal on survival of transplanted sabal palms." *Journal of Arboriculture* 17: 32-33.

Broschat, T. K. and H. M. Donselman. 1984a. "Root regeneration in transplanted palms." *Principes* 28: 90-91.

Broschat, T. K. and H. M. Donselman. 1984b. "Regrowth of severed palm roots." *Journal of Arboriculture* 10: 238-240.

Broschat, T. K. and H. M. Donselman. 1986. "Factors affecting palm transplant success." *Proc. Fl. State Hort. Soc.* 100: 396-397.

Broschat, and H. M. Donselman. 1990. "Regeneration of severed roots in Washingtonia robusta and Phoenix reclinata." *Principes* 34: 96-97.

Meerow, A. W. and T. K. Broschat. 1992. "Transplanting Palms." *University of Florida Extension Circular 1047.*

Cold Protection And Treating Cold-Damaged Palms

Cold temperatures slow the growth rate of palms, reduce root activity, and may weaken the plant enough to make it more susceptible to disease. Palms that have received balanced fertilization in the months leading up to the period of coldest temperatures are much more likely to survive and recover from cold damage than nutritionally deficient palms. Frosts and freezing temperatures will kill the foliage of many palm species, and can reduce the function of water conducting tissue in the trunk. For just a small number of valuable palms, and especially if they are not yet too tall, coverage with burlap, sheets, or one of several fabrics available for this purpose may provide adequate protection. Anti-transpirants applied to the foliage may also help, but current research has not yet indicated that these chemicals provide significant cold protection. Tender palms have also been adequately protected by tying up the leaves in a bundle over the bud. Icing the plants with overhead irrigation works well if performed properly. The irrigation must be turned on before temperatures reach freezing and should continue until the ice visibly melts from the plant surfaces and temperatures rise above freezing. The weight of the ice can, however, cause breakage of palm leaves.

If the irreplaceable bud or "palm heart" survives exposure to freezing temperatures, the recovery of the plant is possible, but proper care in the first few weeks after damage is essential. Leaves with any amount of green tissue should be left on the plants. It may even be wise to leave completely dead leaves attached until the danger of further cold weather is past, since they will provide some measure of insulation to the growing bud.

If the emerging spear is obviously damaged, it should be tugged upon gently to see if it will pull freely from the bud. If it comes free, the hollow collar of sheathing leaf bases that remains should be cleaned out with water. A drainage hole should be carefully made at the base of this collar so that water does not accumulate inside and potentially lead to the rot of the growing point. Some palm growers cut this collar back to a point just above solid tissue. This has the same effect as piercing the base, but does eliminate potential insulation around the tender bud in the event of further cold exposure.

Application of fungicide to the remaining foliage and bud immediately after damage and again 7 to 10 days later may help reduce further loss to disease. Copper based chemicals have traditionally been used for this purpose, but few are currently labelled for palms. Copper sprays should not be repeated more than twice because of the possibility of copper phytotoxicity.

If healthy leaves are present on the palms, or as soon as new leaves emerge, a foliar fertilization with a soluble micronutrient mix should be applied and repeated at monthly intervals until new growth is well under way. A complete fertilizer should be soil applied if this had not been done recently.

Possible Preventative Action

The secondary plant pathogens that cause death of the bud soon after freeze damage are likely bacteria present on healthy palm tissue at low levels, but become a problem only after the damage is received. Consequently, there may be value in applying a preventative spray of fungicidal copper BEFORE freezing temperatures are reached in order to reduce these bacteria populations to the lowest levels possible. This strategy has not been tested, however, under controlled conditions.

Cryptic Cold Damage

Palms that were severely damaged during the winter should be watched carefully during the subsequent spring and summer seasons. Damage to embryonic leaves within the bud may not show up until those leaves emerge (as much as 6 months to 1 year after the freeze). If leaves emerging during the spring and summer months appear deformed, partially browned or otherwise abnormal, this may be indicative of this type of damage. In most cases, the palm will grow out of this later in the season. As the palm grows further, it may be noticed that the trunk is abnormally constricted just below the crown. Such constrictions occur as a consequence of environmental stress, including cold damage.

Freeze damage to conducting tissue in the trunk may limit the ability of the palm to supply water to the canopy of leaves. Unlike typical broad-leafed trees, palms have no ability to regenerate conducting tissue in the trunk. Sudden collapse of some (or even all) of the leaves in the crown during the first periods of high temperature in the spring or summer after a winter freeze may indicate that this type of trunk damage has occurred. Unfortunately, there is nothing that can be done to remedy this, and loss of the palm may be inevitable.

Insect Pests Of Landscape Palms

We are fortunate indeed that, relative to many other landscape plants, a well-grown palm remains fairly free of debilitating insect pests. Nevertheless, certain insects will occasionally attack landscape palms in sufficient force to warrant control measures.

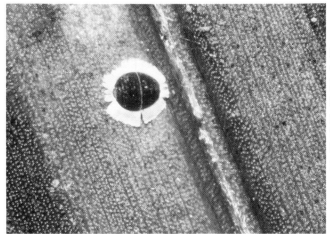

Figure 26. Palm aphid.

Palm aphid (*Cerataphis palmae*). This aphid is unusual in that the female becomes sedentary like a scale, and forms a distinctive ring of white wax around its body (Fig. 26). These aphids heavily infest young leaves and excrete honeydew upon which sooty mold will grow. They are sometimes tended by ants. Dimethoate (Cygon) and Orthene have provided some chemical control. Insecticidal soaps have also effectively controlled these sucking insects. Lady beetles are an excellent biological control, and spraying should be avoided if these aphid predators are observed on the infested palm.

Scales, in great variety, do turn up on palm leaves from time to time, including thread scale, magnolia white scale (Fig. 27), oyster scale, Florida red scale (Fig. 28) and others. The hard shell of many scales reduces the effectiveness of many chemicals. Dimethoate (Cygon) has worked reasonably well on a variety of these troublesome pests. Supracide is currently considered by many growers to be the most effective chemical control. Although a number of beneficial insect predators for scales are available from commercial firms dealing in predatory insects, there is not a great deal of information on the relative effectiveness of these scale "eaters."

Figure 27. Magnolia white scale.

Figure 28. Florida red scale.

Spider mites. Spider mites are particularly a problem on greenhouse grown indoor palms, and on many *Chamaedorea* species. The predatory mite species, *Phytoseiulus persimilis* has been very successfully used to control two-spotted mites (*Tetranychus urticae*) on palms in the greenhouse environment and interiorscapes as well. Many chemical miticides also work successfully.

Coconut mite. This tiny mite feeds on the husk of coconut fruits, causing mostly cosmetic damage (Fig. 29) but sometimes premature fruit drop as well.

Banana moth (*Opogona sacchari*). The larvae of this moth has been a destructive pest on a number of palm species in tropical areas, especially *Chamaedorea* species and arecas. Though more a palm production pest, infestations of landscape palms have occurred. The caterpillar tunnels through the stems of the palms. Lindane and Sevin have had some success in control, and Dipel may be effective as well. Parasitic nematodes have also been fairly effective in controlling infestations of this insect.

Figure 29. Coconut fruits disfigured by coconut mites.

Figure 30. Damage caused by palm leaf skeletonizer.

Palm leaf skeletonizer (*Homaledra sabalella*). The caterpillars of this small moth feed on the upper and lower leaf surfaces of many palms, producing large quantities of "frass" (fibrous excrement) that is often the first conspicuous sign of an infestation (Fig. 30). The tissue between the veins or ribs is usually their preferred food, but they will also feed on the leaf stems, disrupting the vascular tissue and causing the death of the entire leaf. No one control has been reported to be supremely effective. Sevin, Lindane and the biopesticide Dipel 2X have all had some success.

Royal palm bug (*Xylastodoris luteolus*, Fig. 31) is a troublesome pest of royal palms (*Roystonea* species) in Florida and the Caribbean. Infestations in south Florida tend to increase in the spring and summer following a particularly mild winter. This tiny bug feeds on the young leaves of the palms (Fig. 32), often getting in between the folds of an emerging leaf. When the leaf unfolds it appears scorched and brown, and usually fails to mature. A foliar spray with dimethoate (Cygon) has been found to be the best control, though application to very tall royal palms can be problematic.

Figure 31. Royal palm bugs.

Palmetto weevils (*Rynchophorus cruentatus*) are large beetles that are drawn to stressed palms in the subtropical deep south (Fig. 33). They most frequently attack cabbage palms (*Sabal palmetto*) and Canary Island date palms (*Phoenix canariensis*), but have been reported on Mexican fan palms (*Washingtonia robusta*), Bismarck palms (*Bismarckia nobilis*) and latan palms (*Latania* spp.) Adult females lay eggs in the leaf bases of the crown, and the large larvae (Fig. 34) quickly tunnel into the heart, destroying the palm. The crowns of affected palms frequently topple over or "deadhead" (Fig. 35). All efforts should be made to reduce transplant stress on susceptible species. A preventative spray of either Lindane or Dursban, applied at and again a few weeks after installation, has shown some success in keeping palms free of infestation. A related species, *R. palmarum*, occurs in Central and South America and the Caribbean and spreads a destructive nematode that causes red ring disease in coconuts and African oil palms.

Figure 32. Damage caused by royal palm bug.

Figure 33. Adult female palmetto weevils.

Figure 35. "Deadheading" of cabbage palm (*Sabal palmetto*) caused by palmetto weevils.

Figure 34. Larva of palmetto weevil and typical feeding damage.

Various caterpillars (Fig. 36) and some grasshoppers feed on the leaves of palms from time to time. Small infestations can be dealt with mechanically without recourse to pesticides; however, if these insects are on palm foliage in force, they can very quickly do appreciable damage, completely defoliating a young palm in as little as 1-2 days. The biopesticide Dipel 2X is effective on a wide variety of caterpillars. Dursban or Lindane will control grasshoppers if treatment is applied when the insects are young.

Figure 36. Stinging saddleback caterpillar.

Disease Problems Of Palms

Leaf Spots

A number of leaf spot fungi cause variously shaped lesions on the leaf surface of many palm species. High rainfall or frequent overhead irrigation are often instrumental in their spread. If only a single leaf is affected, removal and disposal of that leaf is a simple and effective control. Some leaf spot fungi move in as secondary problems on palm leaves that are deficient in nutrients or have received some sort of damage.

Figure 37. Helminthosporium-complex leaf spot.

Figure 38. Graphiola false smut.

Leaf spot diseases caused by various *Bipolaris* and *Exserohilum* fungi (often called **Helminthosporium-complex** leaf spots) affect a broad range of palms with characteristically round, dark brown lesions (Fig. 37) that eventually merge and form large blighted areas. The disease is easily spread by overhead irrigation. Chlorothalonil and mancozeb fungicides have provided good controls. *Cercospora* leaf spot is frequently a problem on *Rhapis* palms, and *Cylindricladium* on kentia (*Howea forsteriana*). **Anthracnose** caused by a *Colletotrichum* fungus can affect a large number of palms, particularly where overhead irrigation is used. **Stigmina** (*Exosporium* fungus) leaf spot can be a particular problem on date palm (*Phoenix*) species. *Graphiola* **leaf spot** or **"false smut"** can become a significant problem on landscape palms during periods of high rainfall. The disease becomes conspicuous when the fungus responsible produces its grayish-black fruiting bodies which rupture through both leaf surfaces (Fig. 38). Copper based fungicides and maneb or mancozeb have halted infections if applied in the early stages. *Pestalotiopsis* **leaf spot** affects a number of species. It seems to be a particular problem on date palm (*Phoenix*) species on which lesions often first appear on the rachis tissue.

Tar spot (*Catacauma* **leaf spot**) causes elongated, diamond-shaped lesions on the leaf surface. Both copper and a wide range of fungicides have been used to combat this fungal disease. In California and Arizona, **diamond scale** (*Sphaerodothus neowashingtoniae*) attacks California fan palm (*Washingtonia filifera*), causing premature death of the leaves. This fungus produces black, diamond-shaped sporulating structures on the leaf blade and stem. Removing infected leaves is the best control; the effectiveness of fungicides is not reported.

Sooty Mold

This superficial fungal disease (Fig. 39), caused by *Capnodium* spp., is more a nuisance than a life-or-death problem on palms. When present, it is always associated with infestations of sucking insects such as palm aphid, scales, or mealybugs. These insects excrete "honeydew," a waste product high in sugars that the sooty mold fungus feeds upon. The fungus appears on the leaf surface (and sometimes the trunk) as a conspicuous black, sooty deposit. Heavy infestations will interfere with the food-manufacturing efficiency of the leaf. The best control is to keep the palm free of honeydew-producing insects.

Figure 39. Sooty mold.

Bud, Root or Trunk Rots and Wilts

Phytophthora **bud rot** is one of the more common diseases encountered in palms in wet tropical climates (Table 1). It is primarily a warm season disease. This soilborne fungus causes collapse or brown-out of the younger foliage and emerging leaf (Fig. 40). Discoloration of the internal tissue of the stem is evident (Fig. 41), often accompanied by a foul smell. *Phytophthora* can also cause a leaf spot. Good control of bud rot is accomplished by drenching the soil with metalaxyl (Subdue), or applying a foliar spray of fosetyl aluminum (Alliette) at label rate. Foliar applied fosetyl aluminum will translocate to the roots of the palm, whereas metalaxyl will reduce populations of this soil-borne fungus in the root zone. Overwatering and planting too deeply aggravate incidences of *Phytophthora*.

Pink rot or *Gliocladium* **blight**. This fungal disease is a serious problem on *Chamaedorea* species and areca palms in Florida, and queen, date and *Washingtonia* palms in California. The causal agent is not active at temperatures above 85° F, thus it is primarily a winter disease in Florida, while remaining active most of the year in coastal California. Oozing lesions occur on the stems, and leaves turn brown and droop (Fig. 42). The fungus produces salmon-pink, powdery fruiting bodies. The dis-

Figure 40. *Phytophthora* bud rot of coconut (*Cocos nucifera*).

Figure 41. Root rot and discoloration of vascular tissue caused by *Phytophthora*.

Figure 42. Pink rot or *Gliocladium* blight.

Figure 43. Decline of coconut (*Cocos nucifera*) caused by *Ganoderma.*

ease is easily spread if affected leaves are pulled off the plant prematurely, thus leaving an entrance for new disease inoculum. Mancozeb fungicides provide good control.

***Thielaviopsis* trunk** or **bud rot** is increasing in frequency on palms in Florida, but is not yet terribly common. This soil borne fungus generally enters the palm through wounds, and causes the disintegration of the trunk or bud. It can also infect leaves of young palms. A cross-section through the trunk will reveal blackened fruiting bodies. Affected palms will blow over easily.

***Ganoderma* butt rot** has become a serious and incurable disease of older landscape palms (usually 15 or more years old). The disease progresses from the older leaves upward, which turn brown and droop from the trunk (Fig. 43). Wounds on the lower portions of the trunk or roots favor entry of the fungus. The fruiting body of the fungus is a conspicuous bracket or "conch" (Fig. 44). The disease spreads rapidly from plant to plant, and the fungus can persist in the soil for many years. Affected palms must be completely removed and destroyed and the soil fumigated. All visible conchs should be collected and destroyed. If ganoderma has been diagnosed in a landscape site, it may be best to replant with a broad-leafed tree, as no palm can yet be declared reliably resistant.

***Fusarium* wilt** is a problem in California. It may be becoming established in Florida. The disease frequently causes an uneven decline in the canopy of an infected palm, with leaflets on only one side of a single leaf dying first. The water and food conducting tissue within the leaves is usually discolored. Date palms have been the worst affected in California (Fig. 45), while coconuts and Mexican fan palms have reportedly succumbed to this incurable disease in Florida recently. Pruning tools are known to transfer the fungus from tree to tree, and should be sterilized before using again on a different tree.

Bacterial bud rot causes a wet blight of the emerging spear leaf which can spread downward to the irreplaceable bud. Affected spear leaves often will pull easily from the bud. A foul odor frequently accompanies the damage. It often follows hard on the heels of recent cold damage to a palm. Bud drenches with copper-based fungicides have been a common treatment for bacterial bud rots, but their effectiveness has never been absolutely proven.

Figure 44. "Conch" of *Gliocladium* fungus on trunk of affected palm.

Figure 45. Canary Island date palms (*Phoenix canariensis*) with *Fusarium* wilt (left).

Figure 46. Necrotic inflorescence, an early sign of lethal yellowing.

Figure 47. Coconut palm (*Cocos nucifera*) with lethal yellowing.

Lethal Yellowing (LY)

Lethal yellowing is an incurable disease of many palm species caused by a mycoplasma-like organism (a form of life sometimes described as intermediate between a virus and a bacterium) vectored by a leaf hopper bug (*Myndus crudus*). The disease organism is now resident in at least Palm Beach, Broward, Dade, Monroe, Lee and Collier counties of Florida, southern Texas, Mexico, and parts of Africa. The disease often begins with the blackening of young inflorescences on infected palms (Fig. 46). On coconuts, developing fruits will suddenly drop off the stems. One by one, mature leaves may begin to yellow on the palm, until all leaves in the canopy wilt and die (Fig. 47). On other species (and some varieties of coconut as well) the yellowing may not be conspicuous; instead, leaves collapse and the palm quickly dies (Fig. 48). The only practical control is to avoid planting highly LY susceptible palms (Table 2). The decline caused by the disease can be temporarily suspended (though not cured) with a program of injections of tetracycline antibiotics (Fig. 49), but only on palms with a developed trunk. Injections can be maintained until a resistant replacement palm achieves acceptable size, after which the infected palm is allowed to die.

Figure 48. Christmas palm (*Veitchia merrillii*) with lethal yellowing.

Figure 49. Injection of antibiotic into trunk of coconut with lethal yellowing.

Miscellaneous Palm Problems

Landscape palms occasionally experience other problems that are not necessarily the consequences of pests, diseases or nutritional deficiency.

Trunk splits or cracks. Some palm species characteristically develop vertical fissures on their trunks. When these appear on palms that normally do not express them, it is usually an indication of water problems. Both too much or too little soil moisture can result in small cracks on the trunk, as can overly deep planting. Large scale trunk splitting is often associated with an over-abundance of water. Trunk cracking can also occur as a consequence of cold damage.

Trunk constrictions. At the point along their length where active growth is taking place, palm stems complete their caliper growth (that is, increase in diameter) before elongating. The optimal caliper that a palm species will achieve is partially determined by the intrinsic character of the species and partially by the quality of the growing conditions at that point in time. If nutrition or water supply is limiting, or if some other type of environmental stress occurs (a freeze, for example), the palm stem may fail to achieve the same increase in diameter as occurred in past years. As conditions improve, the stem will once again reach optimum caliper. The result over the long term will be a constriction in the trunk at the point where the stem was actively growing when the stresses occurred (Fig. 50). In older palms, it is sometimes possible to "read" the past history of growing conditions by the patterns of constrictions that appear along the length of the trunk.

Pencil-pointing. This syndrome is often related to that of trunk constriction. "Pencil-pointing" refers to a sudden, unnatural narrowing of the stem towards the crown of the palm. It is often associated with

Figure 50. Trunk constriction.

acute nutrient deficiencies, but can also be caused by continuous overtrimming of the canopy. If conditions improve, the palm will return to its normal caliper growth, and a trunk constriction will develop at the point where pencil-pointing was observed.

Figure 51. Lightning strike on coconut palm.

Lightning strike. A direct lightning hit on a palm is usually fatal. Sudden collapse of the crown (Fig. 51), trunk splitting and/or bleeding (Fig. 52), and dark streaks on the trunk are all possible symptoms of lightning damage.

Powerline decline. Tall palms that have reached close proximity to high voltage powerlines have been observed with yellowed or necrotic leaves despite regular fertilization and no evidence of pests or disease, suggesting that the electromagnetic fields around these lines can injure them.

Herbicide toxicity. Many herbicides can cause damage to palms. Telltale signs of herbicide injury include distorted and under-sized new growth and patches of dead tissue on the leaves. Damage from some pre-emergent herbicides may take months to become apparent.

Figure 52. Trunk bleeding caused by lightning strike.

Consequently, special care should taken when using weed-killing chemicals around landscape palms, avoiding any contact of the chemical with new roots, or any green tissue on the palm. Only herbicides labeled for use around palms should be applied.

After-flower decline. Certain palm species (fishtail palms, *Caryota* spp., for example) flower and fruit once and then die. On clustering species with this habit, new stems are produced that continue the growth of the palm, while solitary palms will have to be replaced.

Salt injury. Leaf burn on the windward side of palms planted near the shore is often indicative of salt injury. It usually follows a period of high winds. A sudden intrusion of salt water into the root zone of palms can cause an overall decline and death of the plant. The best way to deal with this problem is to plant in exposed coastal locations only those palms with high salt tolerance.

Table 1. List of palms particularly susceptible to *Phytophthora* bud rot.

Scientific Name	Common Name
Archontophoenix alexandrae	Alexandra palm
Borassus flabellifer	Lontar palm
Brahea armata	Blue hesper palm
Brahea edulis	Guadalupe palm
Butia capitata	Pindo palm
Chamaedorea elegans	Parlor palm
Chamaedorea erumpens	Bamboo palm
Chamaedorea seifrizii	Reed palm
Chrysalidocarpus lutescens	Areca palm
Coccothrinax argentata	Silver palm
Coccothrinax crinita	Old man palm
Cocos nucifera	Coconut palm
Howea forsteriana	Kentia palm
Livistona rotundifolia	Round leaf fan palm
Phoenix canariensis	Canary Island date
Ptychosperma macarthuri	Macarthur palm
Roystonea elata	Florida royal palm
Roystonea regia	Cuban royal palm
Syagrus romanzoffiana	Queen palm
Trachycarpus fortunei	Chusan palm
Trithrinax acanthocoma	Spiny fiber palm
Washingtonia filifera	Petticoat palm
Washingtonia robusta	Washington palm

Table 2. List of some ornamental palms relatively susceptible to lethal yellowing.

Scientific Name	Common Name	Susceptibility
Allagoptera arenaria	Seashore palm	SLIGHT
Arenga engleri	Dwarf sugar palm	HIGH
Borassus flabellifer	Palmyra palm	MODERATE
Caryota mitis	Clustering fishtail palm	MODERATE
C. rumphiana	Solitary fishtail palm	MODERATE
C. urens	Toddy fishtail palm	MODERATE
Chrysalidocarpus cabadae	Cabada palm	SLIGHT
Cocos nucifera*	Coconut	HIGH
Corypha elata	Gebang palm	HIGH
Dictyosperma album	Princess palm	MODERATE
Hyophorbe verschaffeltii	Spindle palm	SLIGHT
Latania spp.	Latan palms	MODERATE
Livistona chinensis	Chinese fan palm	MODERATE
Livistona rotundifolia	Footstool palm	MODERATE
Nannorrhops ritchiana	Mazari palm	SLIGHT
Neodypsis decaryi	Triangle palm	SLIGHT
Phoenix canariensis	Canary Island date	MODERATE
P. dactylifera	Date palm	MODERATE
P. reclinata	Senegal date palm	SLIGHT
Pritchardia spp.	Pritchardia	HIGH
Syagrus schizophylla	Arikury palm	MODERATE
Trachycarpus fortunei	Windmill palm	MODERATE
Veitchia arecina	Arecina palm	SLIGHT
V. merrilli	Christmas palm	HIGH
V. montgomeryana	Montgomery palm	SLIGHT

*resistant varieties available

References

Chase, A. R. and T. K. Broschat (editors). 1991. *Diseases and Disorders of Ornamental Palms.* American Phytopathological Press, St. Paul.

Key To Landscape Palms

How to Use This Key

The following simple key allows the identification of the 102 palm species detailed in this book by growth habit, stem and leaf characteristics only. Technical botanical terms have been avoided or else are "translated" within brackets following their use. Each step of the key consists of a couplet bearing the same number but labeled "a" or "b". Each half of the couplet represents an alternative state for some feature of palm growth or form. Choose the one of the two alternatives that best matches the palm for which identification is desired. Each half of a couplet terminates in either a species name or a number. The number directs you to the next couplet of interest in your search. Continue in this manner until you reach a couplet that terminates in a species name. Use the Main Key first to direct your search to one of the four group keys (A through D). Some palms appear twice in the key due to variation for an important character in that species.

WARNING! This key has been designed to work with palms of sufficient age to have developed mature characteristics. Success may be very limited with young plants.

1a. Leaves pinnately compound, bipinnately compound or simple but two-lobed
   [feather-leafed palms and *Chamaedorea metallica*] 2
1b. Leaves palmate or costapalmate [fan-leafed palms] 3
2a. Leaves pinnately compound or bipinnately compound [feather-leafed palms]..4
2b. Leaves simple but 2-lobed.. *Chamaedorea metallica*
3a. Leaves palmate [fan-leafed palms with no extension of leaf stem into leaf blade].. Key A
3b. Leaves costapalmate [fan-leafed palms with extension of leaf stem into leaf blade] ....Key B
4a. Leaves pinnately compound or bipinnately compound and induplicate
   [feather-leafed palms with leaflet folded upward along midrib: "V"]..Key C
4b. Leaves pinnately compound and reduplicate [feather-leafed palms with leaflet folded downward along midrib: "Λ"] .... Key D

Key A

Palmate palms [fan palms with no extension of leaf stem into leaf blade]

1a. Leaves reduplicate [segments folded downward along midrib: "Λ"]..2
1b. Leaves induplicate [segments folded upward along midrib: "V"] 3
2a. Leaves divided into 4-10 segments bluntly toothed at tips.. *Rhapis excelsa*
2b. Leaves divided into 15-20 nearly pointed segments .... *Rhapis humilis*
3a. Palm clustering 4
3b. Palm solitary..9
4a. Margins of petiole [leaf stem] toothed; stems without spiny fibers 5
4b. Margins of petiole [leaf stem] smooth; stems with persistent, spiny fibers 8
5a. Segments of leaf wedge-shaped and toothed at the blunt tips ....*Licuala spinosa*
5b. Segments of leaf tapering to a pointed, split tip 6
6a. Palm essentially trunkless, prostrate; marginal teeth on leaf stem fine and small, very close together .... *Serenoa repens*
6b. Palm with distinct aerial trunks; marginal teeth coarse, large and more widely spaced 7
7a. Stems slender, 6" or less in diameter ....*Acoelorraphe wrightii*
7b. Stems 6-12" in diameter ....*Chamaerops humilis*
8a. Palm essentially trunkless, rarely more than 6' tall; leaf divided into 15-20 blunt-and-jagged-tipped segments..
   ....*Rhapidophyllum hystrix*
8b. Palm with numerous aerial stems to 15' in height; leaf divided into 30 or more pointed and split segments........*Zombia antillarum*
9a. Margins of petiole [leaf stem] toothed..10
9b. Margins of petiole [leaf stem] smooth..12
10a. Leaf undivided, circular in outline.. *Licuala grandis*
10b. Leaf divided more than halfway into numerous segments, not forming a complete circle in outline 11
11a. Leaves blue-green and densely covered with wax; teeth on petiole [leaf stem] margin large, sharp, curved and black ....
   ....*Copernicia prunifera*
11b. Leaves deep green above, silvery below; teeth on petiole small, round-tipped, and green ....*Trachycarpus fortunei*

12a. Stem covered with persistent spiny fibers ....*Trithrinax acanthocoma*
12b. Stem fibers not spiny 13
13a. Leaf stem bases split where they sheath trunk...14
13b. Leaf stem bases not split..15
14a. Underside of leaf pale green .... *Thrinax radiata*
14b. Underside of leaf silvery-white ....*Thrinax morrissii*
15a. Stem densely covered with very long straw colored hair-like fiber ....*Coccothrinax crinita*
15b. Stem fiber, if present, short and matted...16
16a. Palm usually under 15' in height; petiole [leaf stem] 2.5' long or less; leaf densely silver on underside, segments 1" wide ....
....*Coccothinax argentata*
16b. Palm usually growing to more than 15' in height; petiole 3' or more long; leaf lightly silver on underside, segments 2" wide 17
17a. Canopy of 12-15 leaves ....*Coccothrinax alta*
17b. Canopy of 20-30 leaves ....*Coccothrinax miraguama*

Key B

Costapalmate leafed palms [fan-leafed palms with extension of leaf stem into leaf blade]

1a. Stem solitary 2
1b. Stems clustering...25
2a. Petiole [leaf stem] absent or short and inconspicuous..3
2b. Petiole present 4
3a. Plant to 30' tall; canopy of 20-30 leaves; leaves blue-green, divided into 18-30 segments ....*Copernicia hospita*
3b. Plant to 15' tall; canopy of 12-15 leaves; leaves green, divided into about 60 segments........................... *Copernicia macroglossa*
4a. Petiole without marginal teeth, or teeth sparse and inconspicuous 5
4b. Petiole armed with marginal teeth..14
5a. Base of petiole shortly winged 6
5b. Base of petiole not winged 8
6a. Leaf stem bases smooth and waxy; leaves stiff and upright, to 10' wide, margins of segments not toothed on young plants; hastula
   (see glossary) lopsided ....*Bismarckia nobilis*
6b. Leaf stem bases covered with short, scurfy scales; leaves stiffly folded, 6-8' wide, margins of segments finely toothed on young
   plants; hastula not lop-sided 7
7a. Leaf scars wavy and narrow; leaves entirely blue-green with dense deposit of waxy scurf on underside; hastula pointed and flat....
   ....*Latania loddigesii*[1]
7b. Leaf scars wide, not wavy; leaves gray-green with red margins, lightly or sparsely covered with scurf on underside; hastula
   broad, blunt and raised ....*Latantia lontarioides*[1]
8a. Lower half of all leaf segments regularly drooping or pendent...9
8b. Lower half of all leaf segments not regularly drooping or pendent 10
9a. Plant 25' tall or less; lower half of leaflets pendent at 90° angle from rest of leaf................................*Livistona chinensis*[1]
9b. Plant to 40' tall; lower half of leaflets drooping but at less than 90° angle from rest of leaf ....*Livistona australis*[1]
10a. Leaves divided halfway or more, flat or folded and twisted downward at middle, dull-green or blue-green................11
10b. Leaves divided less than halfway, cupped or folded slightly upward; bright, slightly shiny green...............................13
11a. Trunk massive, several feet in diameter ....*Sabal causiarum*
11b. Trunk about 1' in diameter or absent 12
12a. Plant to 6' tall, trunkless; leaves only shortly costapalmate, flat or slightly folded downward...........................*Sabal minor*
12b. Plant to 40' or more tall; aerial trunk present; leaves deeply costapalmate, folded sharply downward at middle........*Sabal palmetto*
13a. Petiole waxy white; leaves conspicuously cupped upward, divided about 1/4 ....*Pritchardia pacifica*
13b. Petiole green; leaves only slightly folded upward, divided to between 1/4 and 1/2 ....*Pritchardia thurstonii*
14a. Trunk branching above ground..*Hyphaenae* spp.
14b. Trunk unbranched..15
15a. Leaves with fine threads between segments...16
15b. Leaves without fine threads between segments..17
16a. Palm to 100' tall, trunk gray, swollen at base, between 1 and 2 feet in diameter; leaves bright green ....*Washingtonia robusta*
16b. Palm to 50' tall; trunk 2' or more in diameter, brown, not swollen at base; leaves gray-green........................*Washingtonia filifera*
17a. Leaves very stiff, segments not drooping 18
17b. Leaves moderately or slightly stiff, at least some segments drooping 22

18a. Leaves stiffly folded 19
18b. Leaves not stiffly folded 21
19a. Leaf bases split .... *Borassus flabellifer*
19b. Leaf bases not split 20
20a. Leaves blue green, waxy, with 30-40 segments ....*Brahea armata*
20b. Leaves green on both sides with 70-80 segments ....*Brahea edulis*
21a. Leaf scars inconspicuous on trunk; leaves 5' wide ....*Copernicia baileyana*
21b. Trunk ringed with spiraled, swollen leaf scars; leaves 12-18' wide ....*Corypha elata*
22a. Leaves glossy green; segments mostly straight ....*Livistona rotundifolia*
22b. Leaves not glossy green; segments always drooping 23
23a. Leaf segments narrow (< 1" wide), pendent for several feet ....*Livistona decipiens*
23b. Leaf segments at least 2" wide, drooping but not pendent for several feet 24
24a. Leaves divided to more than half their depth, 6' or more wide ....*Livistona mariae*
24b. Leaves divided to mid-depth, 4-5' wide ....*Livistona saribus*
25a. Palm generally 10' tall or less; stems mostly underground, dying back and branching after fruiting; petiole with or without small
     teeth .... *Nannorhops ritchiana*
25b. Palm 15' or more tall; stems aerial and not dying back after flowering; petiole edged with large, sharp teeth ....*Hyphaenae* spp.

[1]Leaf stems of these species are sometimes toothed, usually only in lower half

Key C

Palms with pinnately or bipinnately compound, induplicate leaves
[feather leafed palms with leaflet folded upward along midrib: "V"]

1a. Leaflets on lower portion of rachis [leaf stem extension through leaflets] modified into sharp spines 2
1b. Leaflets not as above 8
2a. Stems solitary..3
2b. Stems clustering...7
3a. Palm 10' tall or less; trunk slender (<1' wide), often thinnest at base..........................*Phoenix roebelenii*
3b. Palm 25' or more tall, trunks at least 1' in diameter, not thinnest at the base.......................................4
4a. Leaf scars not broad nor diamond-shaped ....*Phoenix rupicola*
4b. Leaf scars broad and/or diamond-shaped 5
5a. Trunk 2-3' in diameter; leaves dull green ....*Phoenix canariensis*
5b. Trunk 1-2' in diameter; leaves gray or blue-green...6
6a. Canopy of 20-40 leaves; leaf scars broad but not diamond-shaped ....*Phoenix dactylifera*
6b. Canopy of 50-100 leaves; leaf scars diamond-shaped ....*Phoenix sylvestris*
7a. Stems to 25' tall; trunk slender with ringed leaf scars; leaves dark green ....*Phoenix reclinata*
7b. Stems to 70' tall; trunk robust with broad leaf scars; leaves blue-green ....*Phoenix dactylifera*
8a. Long, spiny fibers persisting on trunk; leaves only once compound; leaflets strap-shaped.............*Arenga pinnata*
8b. Trunk without long spiny fibers; leaves twice compound; leaflets triangular or wedge-shaped 9
9a. Palm clustering ....*Caryota mitis*
9b. Palm solitary..10
10a. Trunk thickest in middle; leaflets triangular, semi-pendulous ....*Caryota rumphiana*
10b. Trunk tapering gradually to apex; leaflets wedge-shaped, pendulous ....*Caryota urens*

Key D

Palms with pinnately compound, reduplicate leaves [feather-leafed palms with leaflet folded downward along midrib: "Λ"]

1a. Leaf bases sheathing tightly and forming a distinct crownshaft..2
1b. Leaf bases not forming a distinct crownshaft or crownshaft loosely formed and not conspicuous..........................28
2a. Crownshaft and leaf stem bright red..*Cyrtostachys renda*
2b. Crownshaft and leaf stem not bright red 3

3a. All or some leaflet tips pointed...4
3b. All leaflet tips blunt and jagged or toothed 18
4a. Palm solitary 5
4b. Palm clustering 15
5a. Leaflets attached in several ranks giving leaf a plume-like appearance...6
5b. Leaflets 2-ranked or forming a "V" in attachment 8
6a. Leaf scars ridged; trunk not swollen above base; leaves arranged in 3 vertical rows ....*Chrysalidocarpus lucubensis*
6b. Leaf scars smooth; trunk usually swollen above base; leaves not arranged in 3 vertical rows........7
7a. Leaflets with conspicuous secondary ribs on either side of midrib.........................*Roystonea regia*
7b. Leaflets without conspicuous secondary ribs on either side of midrib ....*Roystonea elata*
8a. Trunk stout, swollen enormously at base or slightly towards middle; leaf scars smooth 9
8b. Trunk slender; swollen slightly at base if at all; leaf scars ridged...11
9a. Leaves twisted, blue-green; petiole about 2' long..*Pseudophoenix sargentii*
9b. Leaves not twisted, green; petiole no more than 1' long 10
10a. Palm to 12' tall; trunk swollen enormously at base; leaflets held upward in stiff "V" and with secondary ribs..
....*Hyophorbe lagenicaulis*
10b. Palm to 20' tall; trunk swollen towards middle; leaflets held in several planes and without secondary ribs..*Hyophorbe vershaffeltii*
11a. Palm no more than about 10' tall; trunk 1-2" in diameter, producing aerial roots at the nodes [leaf scars]; canopy of 5-7 leaves ..12
11b. Palm 30-40' tall; trunk 6" or more in diameter without aerial roots at ring scars; canopy of 8-20 leaves 13
12a. Leaves 3' or less long; leaflets 6-9" long, about 1" wide.......................................*Chamaedorea elegans*
12b. Leaves to 5' long; leaflets 18-24" long, 1.5-2" wide ....*Chamaedorea tepijilote*[2]
13a. Leaves twisted 90° near tip; crownshaft with dense layer of white or brown woolly scales; leaflets ribbed at margins.................
....*Dictyosperma album*
13b. Leaves not twisted 90° near tip; crownshaft only slightly waxy; leaflets not ribbed at margins 14
14a. Leaflets light green above, grayish-white below, lacking brown woolly scales on underside near midrib ....
....*Archontophoenix alexandrae*
14b. Leaflets green on both sides, with brown, woolly scales on underside near midrib ....*Archontophoenix cunninghamiana*
15a. Leaflets few, broad, the lower ones pointed at tip, the upper ones jagged-toothed at tip ....*Pinanga kuhlii*
15b. Leaflets numerous, narrow, all pointed at tip...16
16a. Palm 60-80' tall; crownshaft bright green; leaflets 1.2-1" wide ....*Euterpe oleracea*
16b. Palm to 30' tall; crownshaft grayish-green; leaflets 1.5" wide...17
17a. Leaves dropping below horizontal; trunk, petiole and rachis yellowish green; leaflets held in narrow "V" ....
....*Chrysalidocarpus lutescens*
17b. Leaves held above the horizontal; trunk bright green; petioles and rachis green or reddish-brown; leaflets held in a lax "V" ....
....*Chrysalidocarpus cabadae*
18a. Leaves with 4-5 dozen leaflets 19
18b. Leaves with 100 or more leaflets...21
19a. Trunk green for many years; terminal 2 leaflets forming a fishtail shape; leaf bases and petioles lacking brown woolly scales ....
....*Areca catechu*
19b. Trunk gray; terminal 2 leaflets not forming a fishtail shape; crownshaft and petioles often with brown woolly scales.................20
20a. Palm solitary; leaflets grayish below ....*Ptychosperma elegans*
20b. Palm clustering; leaflets green on both sides ....*Ptychosperma macarthurii*
21a. Leaflets widest at tip; attached in several planes giving the leaf a plume-like appearance...................*Wodyetia bifurcata*
21b. Leaflets widest at base or middle, attached in 2 ranks 22
22a. Leaf scars very widely spaced on trunk (to 10" apart); uppermost and lower most pairs of leaflets the widest..........................
....*Carpentaria acuminata*
22b. Leaf scars only a few inches apart; uppermost leaflets the narrowest 23
23a. Palm rarely more than 15' tall; leaflets at tip and middle of leaf forming a narrow "V".............*Veitchia merrillii*
23b. Palm generally 25' or more tall; leaflets 2-ranked, sometimes drooping, not held in a "V" 24
24a. Leaflets with fine white scales on underside near midrib..25
24b. Leaflets lacking fine white scales on underside near midrib..26
25a. Leaves with about 90 leaflets ....*Veitchia arecina*
25b. Leaves with 140-160 leaflets...*Veitchia joannis*
26a. Crownshaft with whitish woolly scales near top; older leaves drooping below horizontal ....*Veitchia winin*
26b. Crownshaft with gray or brown woolly scales near top; all leaves held at or above the horizontal 27
27a. Palm to 50' tall; leaves with about 70 leaflets...*Veitchia macdanielsii*
27b. Palm to 35' tall; leaves with 120-140 leaflets.......................................*Veitchia montgomeryana*
28a. Palm clustering 29
28b. Palm solitary...35

29a. Stem, petiole and rachis spiny .... *Bactris gasipaes*
29b. Stem, petiole and rachis unarmed 30
30a. Palm essentially trunkless, stems short; leaf scars inconspicuous 31
30b. Palm with distinct aerial stems and prominent ringed leaf scars 33
31a. Stems with 16-20 leaves; leaflets attached in variously radiating groups of 3, silvery below .... *Allagoptera arenaria*
31b. Stems with 2-8 leaves; leaflets 2-ranked, not silvery below 32
32a. Stems with 2-6 leaves, densely clustering just above the base .... *Chamaedorea cataractarum*
32b. Stems with 6-8 leaves, moderately clustering at the base .... *Chamaedorea radicalis* [3]
33a. Leaves with 16-20 leaflets, 1-2" wide .... *Chamaedorea microspadix*
33b. Leaves with 20-36 leaflets, 1" or less wide 34
34a. Stems with 12-24 leaves .... *Chamaedorea costaricana*
34b. Stems with 6-9 leaves .... *Chamaedorea seifrizii*
35a. Sheathing leaf bases covered with dense, rusty red or brownish-red woolly scurf 36
35b. Leaf bases without dense woolly scurf 37
36a. Leaves radiating out in 3 planes, leaf bases forming a triangular shape; leaflets gray/blue-green, held upward in a "V" ....
.... *Neodypsis decaryi*
36b. Leaves not radiating out in three planes; leaf bases not forming a triangle; leaflets bright green, 2-ranked ...... *Neodypsis lastelliana*
37a. Petiole [leaf stem] with spines or spiny fibers 38
37b. Petiole unarmed 41
38a. Palm to 15' tall; trunk covered with overlapping or spiraled woody leaf base stubs for many years 39
38b. Palm 30-50' tall; trunk clean or with triangular leaf bases in lower portions 40
39a. Leaves (including the petiole) blue green, stiffly arching .... *Butia capitata*
39b. Leaves green, lax; petiole purplish-black .... *Syagrus schizophylla*
40a. Trunk smooth, bearing spines at the ring scars (especially when young); petioles with spines radiating from top and bottom
    surfaces; leaflets with white hairs below .... *Acrocomia aculeata*
40b. Trunk roughened; spiny fibers only along petiole margins; leaflets green on both sides .... *Elaeis guineensis*
41a. Canopy of 5-7 leaves; sheathing leaf base smooth, not fibrous margined or covered with fiber matting, deeply notched on side
    opposite the blade .... *Gaussia maya*
41b. Canopy of 10 or more leaves; sheathing leaf base fibrous margined or covered with fiber matting, not notched 42
42a. Leaflets multi-ranked in radiating groups of 2-7 giving leaves a plume-like appearance .... *Syagrus romanzoffiana*
42b. Leaflets more or less 2-ranked 43
43a. Trunk massive (4-6' in diameter), with diamond shaped leaf scars .... *Jubaea chilensis*
43b. Trunk not more than 2' in diameter; leaf scars not diamond-shaped 44
44a. Trunk with conspicuous crescent-shaped leaf scars; leaf bases covered with fiber matting .... *Cocos nucifera*
44b. Leaf scars not crescent-shaped; leaf bases fibrous margined but not covered with fiber matting 45
45a. Canopy of 20-24 leaves; leaf scars wavy; leaves not twisted .... *Howea forsteriana*
45b. Canopy of 10-16 leaves; leaf scars not wavy; leaves twisted near middle or tip 46
46a. Trunk robust, swollen at base then gradually tapering; leaves twisted near tip .... *Ravenea glauca* or *rivularis*
46b. Trunk slender, swollen at base then tapering quickly; leaves twisted at middle .... *Heterospathe elata*

[2] Clustering forms occur
[3] Forms with aerial stem development occur

SECTION III

USDA Hardiness Zone Map

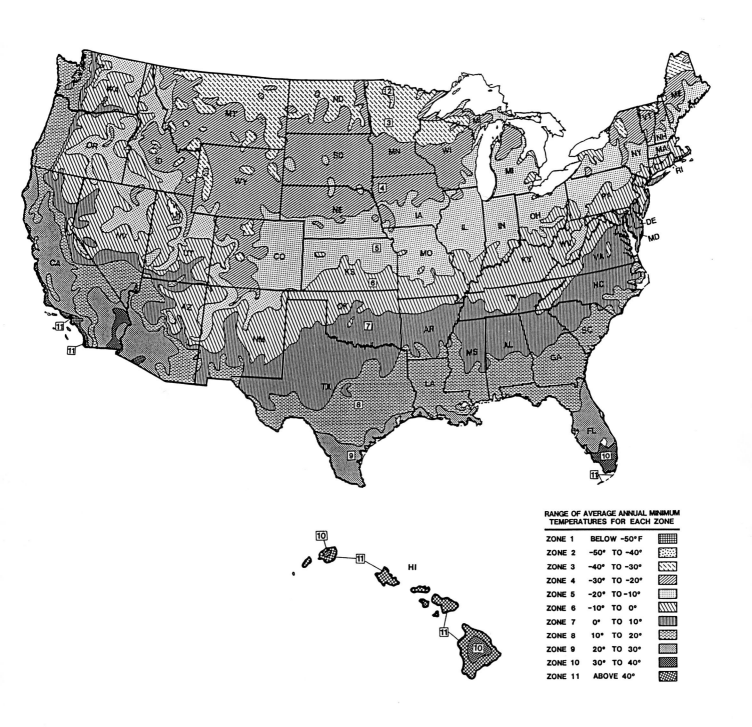

RANGE OF AVERAGE ANNUAL MINIMUM TEMPERATURES FOR EACH ZONE		
ZONE 1	BELOW −50°F	
ZONE 2	−50° TO −40°	
ZONE 3	−40° TO −30°	
ZONE 4	−30° TO −20°	
ZONE 5	−20° TO −10°	
ZONE 6	−10° TO 0°	
ZONE 7	0° TO 10°	
ZONE 8	10° TO 20°	
ZONE 9	20° TO 30°	
ZONE 10	30° TO 40°	
ZONE 11	ABOVE 40°	

Palms Hardy Above USDA Zone 10

	Northernmost Hardiness Zone		Northernmost Hardiness Zone
Acoelorraphe wrightii	9B	Phoenix canariensis	9
Allagoptera arenaria	9B	Phoenix dactylifera	9
Brahea armata	9B	Phoenix sylvestris	9
Butia capitata	8	Rhapidophyllum hystrix	8
Chamaedorea microspadix	9	Sabal causiarum	9B
Chamaedorea radicalis	9	Sabal minor	7
Chamaerops humilis	8	Sabal palmetto	8
Howea forsteriana	9	Serenoa repens	8
Jubaea chilensis	9	Trachycarpus fortunei	8
Livistona australis	9	Trithrinax acanthocoma	9
Livistona chinensis	9	Washingtonia filifera	8
Livistona decipiens	9	Washingtonia robusta	8
Nannorrhops ritchiana	8		

Highly Salt Tolerant Palms

Allagoptera arenaria
Coccothrinax alta
Coccothrinax argentata
Coccothrinax crinita
Coccothrinax miraguama
Cocos nucifera
Hyophorbe lagenicaulis
Hyophorbe verschaffeltii
Hyphaene spp.

Phoenix dactylifera
Pritchardia pacifica
Pritchardia thurstonii
Pseudophoenix sargentii
Sabal palmetto
Serenoa repens
Thrinax morrisii
Thrinax radiata
Zombia antillarum

Highly Drought Tolerant Palms

Acrocomia aculeata
Allagoptera arenaria
Bismarckia nobilis
Borassus flabellifer
Brahea armata
Brahea edulis
Butia capitata
Chrysalidocarpus cabadae
Chrysalidocarpus lutescens
Coccothrinax alta
Coccothrinax argentata
Coccothrinax crinita
Coccothrinax miraguama
Cocos nucifera
Copernicia baileyana
Copernicia hospita
Copernicia macroglossa
Corypha elata
Hyphaene spp.
Latania loddigesii
Latania lontarioides
Livistona australis
Livistona chinensis
Livistona decipiens

Livistona mariae
Livistona saribus
Nannorrhops ritchiana
Phoenix canariensis
Phoenix dactylifera
Phoenix reclinata
Phoenix rupicola
Phoenix sylvestris
Pseudophoenix sargentii
Rhapidophyllum hystrix
Sabal causiarum
Sabal minor
Sabal palmetto
Serenoa repens
Syagrus schizophylla
Thrinax morrisii
Thrinax radiata
Trachycarpus fortunei
Trithrinax acanthocoma
Veitchia winin
Washingtonia filifera
Washingtonia robusta
Zombia antillarum

Palms That Will Grow In Low Light (< 500 foot candles)

Chamaedorea cataractarum
Chamaedorea costaricana
Chamaedorea elegans
Chamaedorea erumpens
Chamaedorea metallica
Chamaedorea microspadix

Chamaedorea radicalis
Chamaedorea seifrizii
Chamaedorea tepejilote
Howea forsteriana
Rhapis excelsa
Rhapis humilis
Sabal minor

Palms That Will Grow Well In Part Shade

Archontophoenix alexandrae
Archontophoenix cunninghamiana
Areca catechu
Arenga tremula
Bactris gasipaes
Bismarckia nobilis
Butia capitata
Caryota mitis
Caryota rumphiana
Chamaedorea cataractarum
Chamaedorea costaricana
Chamaedorea elegans
Chamaedorea erumpens
Chamaedorea metallica
Chamaedorea microspadix
Chamaedorea radicalis
Chamaedorea seifrizii
Chamaedorea tepejilote
Chamaerops humilis
Chrysalidocarpus cabadae
Chrysalidocarpus lucubensis
Chrysalidocarpus lutescens
Coccothrinax alta
Coccothrinax argentata
Coccothrinax crinita
Coccothrinax miraguama
Cyrtostachys renda
Euterpe oleracea
Gaussia maya
Heterospathe elata
Howea forsteriana
Hyophorbe lagenicaulis

Licuala spinosa
Livistona australis
Livistona chinensis
Livistona decipiens
Livistona rotundifolia
Livistona saribus
Neodypsis decaryi
Phoenix roebelenii
Pinanga kuhlii
Pritchardia pacifica
Pritchardia thurstonii
Pseudophoenix sargentii
Ptychosperma elegans
Ptychosperma macarthurii
Ravenea glauca or rivularis
Rhapidophyllum hystrix
Rhapis excelsa
Rhapis humilis
Sabal minor
Serenoa repens
Syagrus romanzoffiana
Syagrus schizophylla
Thrinax morrisii
Thrinax radiata
Trachycarpus fortunei
Veitchia arecina
Veitchia joannis
Veitchia macdanielsii
Veitchia merrillii
Veitchia montgomeryana
Veitchia winin
Wodyetia bifurcata

Fast Growing Palms

Carpentaria acuminata
Caryota rumphiana
Chamaedorea tepejilote
Euterpe oleracea
Syagrus romanzoffiana
Veitchia arecina

Veitchia joannis
Veitchia macdanielsii
Veitchia montgomeryana
Veitchia winin
Washingtonia robusta
Wodyetia bifurcata

Palms Generally 20' Tall Or Less

Acoelorrhaphe wrightii
Allagoptera arenaria
Butia capitata
Caryota mitis
Chamaedorea cataractarum
Chamaedorea costaricana
Chamaedorea elegans
Chamaedorea erumpens
Chamaedorea metallica
Chamaedorea microspadix
Chamaedorea seifrizii
Chamaedorea tepejilote
Chamaerops humilis
Coccothrinax argentata
Coccothrinax crinita
Coccothrinax miraguama
Copernicia macroglossa
Cyrtostachys renda
Hyophorbe lagenicaulis

Hyophorbe verschaffeltii
Hyphaene spp. (some only)
Licuala grandis
Licuala spinosa
Nannorrhops ritchiana (occasionally to 25')
Phoenix roebelenii
Pinanga kuhlii
Pseudophoenix sargentii
Ptychosperma elegans
Ravenea glauca (not rivularis)
Rhapidophyllum hystrix
Sabal minor
Serenoa repens
Syagrus schizophylla
Trithrinax acanthocoma
Thrinax morrissii
Thrinax radiata
Veitchia merrillii (occasionally to 25')
Zombia antillarum

Solitary Palms

Acrocomia aculeata
Archontophoenix alexandrae
Archontophoenix cunninghamiana
Areca catechu
Arenga pinnata
Bismarckia nobilis
Borassus flabellifer
Brahea armata
Brahea edulis
Butia capitata
Carpentaria acuminata
Caryota rumphiana
Caryota urens
Chamaedorea elegans
Chamaedorea metallica
Chamaedorea tepejilote (sometimes clustering)
Chrysalidocarpus lucubensis
Coccothrinax alta
Coccothrinax argentata
Coccothrinax crinita
Coccothrinax miraguama
Cocos nucifera
Copernicia baileyana
Copernicia hospita
Copernicia macroglossa
Copernicia prunifera
Corypha elata
Dictyosperma album
Elaeis guineensis
Gaussia maya
Heterospathe elata
Howea forsteriana
Hyophorbe lagenicaulis
Hyophorbe verschaffeltii
Hyphaene spp. (some)
Jubaea chilensis
Latania loddigesii

Latania lontaroides
Licuala grandis
Livistona australis
Livistona chinensis
Livistona decipiens
Livistona mariae
Livistona rotundifolia
Livistona saribus
Neodypsis decaryi
Neodypsis lastelliana
Phoenix canariensis
Phoenix roebelenii
Phoenix rupicola
Phoenix sylvestris
Pritchardia pacifica
Pseudophoenix sargentii
Ptychosperma elegans
Ravenea glauca or rivularis
Roystonea elata
Roystonea regia
Sabal causiarum
Sabal minor
Sabal palmetto
Syagrus romanzoffiana
Syagrus schizophylla
Thrinax morrisii
Thrinax radiata
Trachycarpus fortunei
Trithrinax acanthocoma
Veitchia arecina
Veitchia joannis
Veitchia macdanielsii
Veitchia merrillii
Veitchia montgomeryana
Veitchia winin
Washingtonia filifera
Washingtonia robusta
Wodyetia bifurcata

Clustering Palms

Acoelorrhaphe wrightii
Allagoptera arenaria
Bactris gasipaes
Caryota mitis
Chamaedorea cataractarum
Chamaedorea costaricana
Chamaedorea erumpens
Chamaedorea microspadix
Chamaedorea radicalis
Chamaedorea seifrizii
Chamaedorea tepejilote (sometimes clustering)
Chamaerops humilis
Chrysalidocarpus cabadae

Chrysalidocarpus lutescens
Cyrtostachys renda
Euterpe oleracea
Hyphaene spp. (some)
Nannorrhops ritchiana
Phoenix dactylifera
Phoenix reclinata
Pinanga kuhlii
Ptychosperma macarthurii
Rhapidophyllum hystrix
Rhapis excelsa
Rhapis humilis
Zombia antillarum

Palms With Spines Or Teeth

Acoelorrhaphe wrightii
Acrocomia aculeata
Arenga pinnata
Bactris gasipaes
Bismarckia nobilis (minor hazard)
Borassus flabellifer
Brahea armata
Brahea edulis
Butia capitata
Chamaerops humilis
Copernicia baileyana
Copernicia hospita
Copernicia macroglossa
Copernicia prunifera
Corypha elata
Elaeis guineensis
Hyphaene spp.
Licuala grandis
Licuala spinosa

Livistona australis (variable)
Livistona chinensis (variable)
Livistona decipiens
Livistona mariae
Livistona rotundifolia
Livistona saribus
Phoenix canariensis
Phoenix dactylifera
Phoenix reclinata
Phoenix roebelenii
Phoenix rupicola
Phoenix sylvestris
Rhapidophyllum hystrix
Serenoa repens
Syagrus schizophylla
Trachycarpus fortunei
Trithrinax acanthocoma
Washingtonia filifera
Washingtonia robusta
Zombia antillarum

Palms With Irritating Fruit

Arenga pinnata
Carpentaria acuminata
Caryota mitis
Caryota rumphiana
Caryota urens
Chamaedorea cataractarum
Chamaedorea costaricana (mildly)
Chamaedorea elegans (mildly)
Chamaedorea erumpens (mildly)

Chamaedorea metallica (mildly)
Chamaedorea microspadix (mildly)
Chamaedorea radicalis (mildly)
Chamaedorea seifrizii (mildly)
Chamaedorea tepejilote
Gaussia maya
Ptychosperma spp. (some)
Roystonea elata
Roystonea regia

Index To Common Names And Synonyms

Common Name or Synonym	Correct Scientific Name
Actinophloeus macarthuri	*Ptychosperma macarthurii*, p. 78
Adonidia	*Veitchia merrillii*, p. 98
African oil palm	*Elaeis guineensis*, p. 45
Alexander palm	*Ptychosperma elegans*, p. 77
Alexandra palm	*Archontophoenix alexandrae*, p. 6
Areca lutescens	*Chrysalidocarpus lutescens*, p. 32
Areca palm	*Chrysalidocarpus lutescens*, p. 32
Arecastrum romanzoffianum	*Syagrus romanzoffiana*, p. 89
Arecina palm	*Veitchia arecina*, p. 95
Arikury palm	*Syagrus schizophylla*, p. 90
Arikuryoba schizophylla	*Syagrus schizophylla*, p. 90
Assai palm	*Euterpe oleracea*, p. 46
Australian fan palm	*Livistona australis*, p. 58
Bailey copernicia	*Copernicia baileyana*, p. 38
Bamboo palm	*Chamaedorea erumpens*, p. 23
Bamboo palm	*Chamaedorea seifrizii*, p. 27
Bangalow palm	*Archontophoenix cunninghamiana*, p. 7
Betelnut palm	*Areca catechu*, p. 8
Bismarck palm	*Bismarckia nobilis*, p. 11
Blue hesper palm	*Brahea armata*, p. 13
Blue latan palm	*Latania loddigesii*, p. 54
Bottle palm	*Hyophorbe lagenicaulis*, p. 50
Buccaneer palm	*Pseudophoenix sargentii*, p. 76
Butterfly palm	*Chrysalidocarpus lutescens*, p. 32
Cabada palm	*Chrysalidocarpus cabadae*, p. 30
Cabbage palm	*Sabal palmetto*, p. 87
California fan palm	*Washingtonia filifera*, p. 101
Canary Island date	*Phoenix canariensis*, p. 67
Carnauba wax palm	*Copernicia prunifera*, p. 41
Carpentaria palm	*Carpentaria acuminata*, p. 16
Cat palm	*Chamaedorea cataractarum*, p. 20
Central Australian fan palm	*Livistona mariae*, p. 61
Chamaedorea tenella	*Chamaedorea metallica*, p. 24
Chamaerops excelsa	*Trachycarpus fortunei*, p. 93
Chilean wine palm	*Jubaea chilensis*, p. 53
Chinese fan palm	*Livistona chinensis*, p. 59
Chinese windmill palm	*Trachycarpus fortunei*, p. 93
Christmas palm	*Veitchia merrillii*, p. 98
Chusan palm	*Trachycarpus fortunei*, p. 93
Cliff date	*Phoenix rupicola*, p. 71
Clustering fishtail palm	*Caryota mitis*, p. 17

Index To Common Names And Synonyms

Common Name or Synonym	Correct Scientific Name
Coconut palm	*Cocos nucifera*, p. 37
Cocos australis	*Syagrus romanzoffiana*, p. 89
Cocos plumosa	*Syagrus romanzoffiana*, p. 89
Collinia elegans	*Chamaedorea elegans*, p. 22
Corypha australis	*Livistona australis*, p. 58
Corypha elata	*Corypha utan*, p. 42
Costa Rican bamboo palm	*Chamaedorea costaricana*, p. 21
Cuban petticoat palm	*Copernicia macroglossa*, p. 40
Cuban royal palm	*Roystonea regia*, p. 84
Cyrtostachys lakka	*Cyrtostachys renda*, p. 43
Date palm	*Phoenix dactylifera*, p. 68
Desert fan palm	*Washingtonia filifera*, p. 101
Dictyosperma rubrum	*Dictyosperma album* var. *aureum*, p. 44
Diplothemium maritimum	*Allagoptera arenaria*, p. 5
Duom palm	*Hyphaene* spp., p. 52
Dwarf palmetto	*Sabal minor*, p. 86
Dwarf sugar palm	*Arenga tremula*, p. 9
European fan palm	*Chamaerops humilis*, p. 29
Erythea armata	*Brahea armata*, p. 13
Everglades palm	*Acoelorrhaphe wrightii*, p. 3
Fiji fan palm	*Pritchardia pacifica*, p. 74
Florida royal palm	*Roystonea elata*, p. 83
Florida thatch palm	*Thrinax radiata*, p. 92
Footstool palm	*Livistona rotundifolia*, p. 62
Foxtail palm	*Wodyetia bifurcata*, p. 103
Gebang palm	*Corypha utan*, p. 42
Giant fishtail palm	*Caryota rumphiana*, p. 18
Gingerbread palm	*Hyphaene* spp., p. 52
Guadalupe palm	*Brahea edulis*, p. 14
Guilielma gasipaes	*Bactris gasipaes*, p. 10
Hardy bamboo palm	*Chamaedorea microspadix*, p. 25
Hat palm	*Sabal causiarum*, p. 85
Hospita palm	*Copernicia hospita*, p. 39
Hurricane palm	*Dictyosperma album*, p. 44
Ivory cane palm	*Pinanga kuhlii*, p. 73
Jaggery palm	*Caryota urens*, p. 19
Jelly palm	*Butia capitata*, p. 15
Joannis palm	*Veitchia joannis*, p. 96
Jubaea spectabilis	*Jubaea chilensis*, p. 53
Kentia acuminata	*Carpentaria acuminata*, p. 16
Kentia forsteriana	*Howea forsteriana*, p. 49

Index To Common Names And Synonyms

Common Name or Synonym	Correct Scientific Name
Kentia palm	*Howea forsteriana*, p. 49
Key thatch palm	*Thrinax morrisii*, p. 91
King Alexander palm	*Archontophoenix alexandrae*, p. 6
Lady palm	*Rhapis excelsa*, p. 81
Latania borbonica	*Latania lontaroides*, p. 55
Latania commersonii	*Latania lontaroides*, p. 55
Licuala palm	*Licuala grandis*, p. 56
Lipstick palm	*Cyrtostachys renda*, p. 43
Livistona cochinchinensis	*Livistona saribus*, p. 63
Livistona oliviformis	*Livistona chinensis*, p. 59
Lontar palm	*Borassus flabellifer*, p. 12
Lucubensis palm	*Chrysalidocarpus lucubensis*, p. 31
Macarthur palm	*Ptychosperma macarthurii*, p. 78
Macaw palm	*Acrocomia aculeata*, p. 4
Majesty palm	*Ravenea glauca* or *rivularis*, p. 79
Manila palm	*Veitchia merrillii*, p. 98
Mascarena lagenicaulis	*Hyophorbe lagenicaulis*, p. 50
Mascarena verschaffeltii	*Hyophorbe verschaffeltii*, p. 51
Maya palm	*Gaussia maya*, p. 47
Mazari palm	*Nannorrhops ritchiana*, p. 64
Mexican fan palm	*Washingtonia robusta*, p. 102
Miniature fishtail palm	*Chamaedorea metallica*, p. 24
Miraguama palm	*Coccothrinax miraguama*, p. 36
Montgomery palm	*Veitchia montgomeryana*, p. 99
Neanthe bella	*Chamaedorea elegans*, p. 22
Needle palm	*Rhapidophyllum hystrix*, p. 80
Old man palm	*Coccothrinax crinita*, p. 35
Opsiandra maya	*Gaussia maya*, p. 47
Oreodoxa regia	*Roystonea regia*, p. 84
Pacaya	*Chamaedorea tepejilote*, p. 28
Palmyra palm	*Borassus flabellifer*, p. 12
Parlor palm	*Chamaedorea elegans*, p. 22
Paurotis palm	*Acoelorrhaphe wrightii*, p. 3
Paurotis wrightii	*Acoelorrhaphe wrightii*, p. 3
Peaberry palm	*Thrinax morrisii*, p. 91
Peach palm	*Bactris gasipaes*, p. 10
Pejibaye	*Bactris gasipaes*, p. 10
Petticoat palm	*Washingtonia filifera*, p. 101
Piccabeen palm	*Archontophoenix cunninghamiana*, p. 7
Pindo palm	*Butia capitata*, p. 15
Princess palm	*Dictyosperma album*, p. 44

Index To Common Names And Synonyms

Common Name or Synonym	Correct Scientific Name
Pygmy date palm	*Phoenix roebelenii*, p. 70
Queen palm	*Syagrus romanzoffiana*, p. 89
Radicalis palm	*Chamaedorea radicalis*, p. 26
Reclinata palm	*Phoenix reclinata*, p. 69
Red latan palm	*Latania lontaroides*, p. 55
Red sealing wax palm	*Cyrtostachys renda*, p. 43
Redneck palm	*Neodypsis lastelliana*, p. 66
Reed palm	*Chamaedorea seifrizii*, p. 27
Rhapis flabelliformis	*Rhapis excelsa*, p. 81
Ribbon fan palm	*Livistona decipiens*, p. 60
Round leaf fan palm	*Livistona rotundifolia*, p. 62
Sabal palm	*Sabal palmetto*, p. 87
Sagisi palm	*Heterospathe elata*, p. 48
Saw palmetto	*Serenoa repens*, p. 88
Seaforthia elegans	*Ptychosperma* elegans, p. 77; *Archontophoenix alexandrae*, p. 6
Seashore palm	*Allagoptera arenaria*, p. 5
Senegal date	*Phoenix reclinata*, p. 69
Sentry Palm	*Howea forsteriana*, p. 49
Silver palm	*Coccothrinax alta*, p. 33
Silver palm	*Coccothrinax argentata*, p. 34
Slender lady palm	*Rhapis humilis*, 82
Solitaire palm	*Ptychosperma elegans*, p. 77
Spindle palm	*Hyophorbe verschaffeltii*, p. 51
Spiny fiber palm	*Trithrinax acanthocoma*, p. 94
Spiny licuala	*Licuala spinosa*, p. 57
Sunshine palm	*Veitchia macdanielsii*, p. 97
Taraw palm	*Livistona saribus*, p. 63
Teddy bear palm	*Neodypsis lastelliana*, p. 66
Thrinax floridana	*Thrinax radiata*, p. 92
Thrinax microcarpa	*Thrinax morrissii*, p. 91
Thurston palm	*Pritchardia thurstonii*, p. 75
Toddy fishtail palm	*Caryota urens*, p. 19
Toddy palm	*Phoenix sylvestris*, p. 72
Triangle palm	*Neodypsis decaryi*, p. 65
Washington palm	*Washingtonia robusta*, p. 102
Wild date palm	*Phoenix sylvestris*, p. 72
Windmill palm	*Trachycarpus fortunei*, p. 93
Winin palm	*Veitchia winin*, p. 100
Zombie palm	*Zombia antillarum*, p. 104

Glossary

adventitious roots: roots originating from stem tissue rather than from other roots; all mature palm roots are adventitious.

armed: bearing spines or teeth.

bipinnately compound: a feather palm leaf that is twice-compound; that is, the primary leaflets themselves consist of system of smaller secondary leaflets.

bract: a hood-like or leaf-like protective structure found at the base of an inflorescence.

chlorosis (chlorotic, adj.): yellowing of plant leaves caused by disease or nutrient deficiency.

costa: the extension of the leaf stem (petiole) into the blade on a costapalmate leaf.

costapalmate: a fan palm leaf with an extension of the leaf stem (petiole) into the blade.

clustering palm: a palm that branches at the base or below and produces several or numerous stems.

crownshaft: a conspicuous neck-like structure formed by the tubular leaf bases of some feather-leafed palms that sheath each other very tightly around the stem.

division: propagation of a clustering palm by splitting the clump.

drupe: a fleshy, one-seeded fruit that doesn't open up at maturity, typical of many palm fruits.

genus (plural: genera): a group of related species believed to be of common ancestry and defined by certain important shared characteristics that set them apart from other species groups.

hastula: a small, thin, more or less rounded protuberance of tissue located at the point where the petiole meets the blade on a fan palm leaf.

induplicate: a palm leaf in which the leaflets or segments are folded upward, forming a "V".

inflorescence: the flower stalk of a plant.

leaf base: the lowest and widest portion of the palm leaf stem or petiole that sheathes the stem.

leaf blade: the upper, expanded portion of a palm leaf.

leaf scar: the mark left behind on a palm trunk at a leaf's point of attachment after the leaf falls.

leaf stem: the petiole of a palm leaf.

marginal reins: long, linear strands of leaf tissue that hang down from the leaf margins of some feather palms. Often attached to the tips of the leaflets when the leaf first unfolds.

necrosis (necrotic, adj.): death of plant tissue in which browning or blackening of the tissue occurs; frequently a symptom of disease, insect damage, nutrient deficiency, or some other type of physiological problem.

node: the point on the stem at which a leaf is attached.

palmate: a fan palm leaf lacking a costa.

palm cabbage: edible palm hearts.

palm heart: the bud or growing point of a palm, including several series of embryonic leaves. Harvested from some species and eaten fresh or cooked.

petiole: the stem of a palm leaf.

pinnately compound: feather palm leaves that are only once-compound; that is, there is only a single series of leaflets.

phloem: food conducting cells in plant tissue.

rachis: the extension of the leaf stem (petiole) through the leaflets of a feather palm.

reduplicate: a palm leaf in which the leaflets or segments are folded downward, forming an inverted "V".

rib: upraised vein on a palm leaf or leaflet.

ring scar: the mark left behind on a palm trunk after a leaf that completely sheathes the stem falls off.

root initiation zone: specialized area at the base of the palm stem from which roots are produced.

scales: short, waxy or woolly hairs that occur on various parts of some palms.

scurf: dense deposits of scales on a palm leaf stem or other part of the palm.

secondary growth: the ability of plant stems and roots to produce new vascular tissue and increase in diameter with age; this ability is lacking in palms.

segment: the split portions of a fan palm leaf.

spathe: a hood-like or boat-shaped bract.

spear: the tightly folded emergent leaf(ves) of a palm.

solitary palm: a palm that produces only one trunk or stem.

subfamily: a subdivision of a plant family which unites genera that all share certain important characteristics and are believed to be of common descent.

tribe: a group of closely related genera within a subfamily.

unarmed: free of spines or teeth.

vascular bundles: columns of water and food conducting cells within the stem of a palm.

vascular tissues: the water and food conducting tissue of a plant.

xylem: water conducting cells in plant tissue.

Selected Bibliography Of Palm Books

Blombery, A. and T. Rodd. 1988. *Palms of the World. Their Cultivation, Care and Landscape Use*. Angus & Robertson, New South Wales.

Braun, A. 1968. "Cultivated Palms of Venezuela." Reprint of *Principes* vol. 12 (2-4). International Palm Society.

Chase, A. R. and T. K. Broschat (editors). 1991. *Diseases and Disorders of Ornamental Palms*. American Phytopathological Press, St. Paul.

Corner, E. J. H. 1966. *The Natural History Of Palms*. Weidenfield and Nicholson, London.

Dowe, J. A. 1989. *Palms of the Southwest Pacific*. Palm and Cycad Societies of Australia, Queensland.

Hodel, D. R. 1992. *Chamaedorea Palms*. International Palm Society, Allen Press, Lawrence, KS.

Jones, D. L. 1985. *Palms In Colour*. Reed Books, New South Wales.

Jones, D. L. 1984. *Palms in Australia*. Reed Books, New South Wales.

Krempin, J. 1990. *Palms and Cycads Around the World*. Horwitz Grahame, Sydney.

Langlois, A. C. 1976. *Supplement to Palms of the World*. University of Florida Press, Gainesville (1980 reprint published by Horticultural Books, Stuart, FL).

McCurrach, J. C. 1960. *Palms of the World*. Harper & Brothers, New York.

Stevenson, G. B. 1974. *Palms of South Florida*. Privately published.

Tomlinson, P. B. 1990. *The Structural Biology of Palms*. Clarendon Press, Oxford.

Uhl, N. W. and J. Dransfield. 1987. *Genera Palmarum*. International Palm Society, Allen Press, Lawrence, KS.

About The Author

Dr. Alan W. Meerow is Associate Professor, Palm and Tropical Ornamentals Specialist at the University of Florida's Fort Lauderdale Research & Education Center, and a research collaborator at Fairchild Tropical Garden. He received his B.S. degree in botany and environmental horticulture from the University of California at Davis and his M.S. and Ph.D from the University of Florida in horticultural science and botany. Dr. Meerow teaches "Palm Production and Culture" and other courses in the Ft. Lauderdale Degree Program in Environmental Horticulture, coordinates the University of Florida's south Florida extension program in commercial ornamentals, and conducts research in various aspects of tropical horticulture and botany. He has been recognized by the Florida Nurserymen and Growers Association as Horticultural Writer of the Year in 1990, and Educator of the Year in 1991. Dr. Meerow is an internationally recognized authority on the amaryllis family and has published numerous scientific papers on the taxonomy of that group. He has published over one hundred scientific, extension, trade and popular magazine articles on plants. He and Dr. Timothy K. Broschat are the authors of *Betrock's Guide to Florida Landscape Plants*. Dr. Meerow resides in Davie, Florida with his wife Linda, and two children, Sara and Andrew.